Training for the 40-Yard Dash

**Michael Barnes
John Cissik**

©2008 Coaches Choice. All rights reserved. Printed in the United States.

No part of this book may be reproduced, stored in a retrieval system, or transmitted, in any form or by any means, electronic, mechanical, photocopying, recording, or otherwise, without the prior permission of Coaches Choice.

ISBN: 978-1-58518-059-2
Library of Congress Control Number: 2007933804

Book layout: Bean Creek Studio
Cover design: Bean Creek Studio
Front cover photo: Brennan Tiffany
Text photos: Michael Barnes

Coaches Choice
P.O. Box 1828
Monterey, CA 93942
www.coacheschoice.com

Dedication

To Sue, Zachary, and Sydney. Why run when you can fly?

—Mike Barnes

Acknowledgments

To attempt to acknowledge the many people that deserve my gratitude would be impossible. The people that I have worked for and with are countless and I have learned something from each of them.

I would like to thank Shane Domer, Keith Cinea, Robin Pound, Eric Hohn, Jerry Attaway, Dwight Clark, George Seifert, Steve Mariucci, Peter Melanson, Steve Plisk, Mike Miller, John Graham, Scott Reiwald, William Kraemer, Dave Sandler, John Taylor, Jay Hoffman, Kevin Clearly, Charles Ash, Ben Reuter, Mark Stephanson, Allen Hedrick, Virginia Meier, Karrie Baker, Tom Hastings, Scott Brone, Avery Faigenbaum, Bob Alejo, Tom Billups, Mike and Lori Chaplin, Jay Dawes, Jeremy Strom, Dave Ellis, Paul Goldberg, Tom Grace, and the hundreds of coaches and athletes that I have had the privilege to work with over many years.

I would like to specifically thank my good friend and co-author, John Cissik. He has inspired me to become a better practitioner and to truly base coaching and education on scientific principles.

—Mike Barnes

Contents

Dedication 3
Acknowledgments 4
Preface 6

Part I: Science
    Chapter 1: Understanding the Basics 7
    Chapter 2: Before Starting a Conditioning Program 13
    Chapter 3: How Everything Works 18

Part II: Application
    Chapter 4: The Start Position 27
    Chapter 5: Acceleration 32
    Chapter 6: Top Speed 35

Part III: Training
    Chapter 7: Training Principles 43
    Chapter 8: Nutrition, Body Composition, and Rest 52
    Chapter 9: Warming Up 59
    Chapter 10: Running Fast to Be Fast 65
    Chapter 11: Strength Training 76
    Chapter 12: Plyometrics 91
    Chapter 13: Staying Healthy 104
    Chapter 14: Sample Developmental Programs 109

About the Authors 122

Preface

The 40-yard dash, or "40," is perhaps the most highly evaluated performance criteria among coaches throughout the country. A good time can determine who makes the high school football team or how high an athlete is selected in the NFL draft. During our years of coaching, we have collected our observations about several aspects of the 40, including biomechanics, weight training, plyometrics, and ultimately running a faster time. It is our pleasure to share these training techniques and tips, which will maximize your training time and give your athletes the best possible results.

This manual is intended for coaches working with athletes who are interested in running a faster 40 time. The majority of high school, collegiate, and professional athletes use the 40 as an off-season or preseason test to determine speed, fitness, improvement, and potentially the ability to play. It has been our observation that many of these athletes do not properly run or train to their potential.

Genetic potential plays a big part of running a fast 40, but with proper technique and training it is not uncommon for an athlete to reduce their 40 time by as much as 0.4 seconds. Some of the strategies that this book covers involve the fundamentals of biomechanics, physiology, the ever-important start position, body composition, weight training, plyometrics, and more.

The contents of the manual are based on science and its practical application. We didn't want to weigh the contents down with lots of cited research, but instead opted to focus on the essential information that would pertain to running the best possible time. The specifics of running the 40 are discussed, as well as assistive training techniques such as weight training and plyometrics. Body composition is critical to running fast as well, and so we decided to include that topic in our discussion of nutrition.

Three different programs are presented in the final chapter of this manual—varsity, All-American, and world class. It is important to note that athletes should only use the program that they are physically ready for and prepared to commit to. The varsity program is for someone who wants to take two to four weeks to clean up their technique and be somewhat prepared to run a decent time. The All American program is for a consistently training athlete who has some training background and is serious about committing several weeks to improving performance. Finally, the world class program is for an athlete who has consistent training habits, at least a year of experience, and must run their personal best. These programs represent our recommendations on exactly how to train for the 40.

If your athletes are committed to improving on a decent time or blowing away the NFL scouts with lightning speed, this manual will accommodate your coaching needs. Good luck.

Part I: Science

1

Understanding the Basics

The 40-yard dash, often simply called "the 40," is a timed sprint over 40 yards. It is measured throughout the United States to determine the speed of athletes, specifically football players. Junior high school, high school, collegiate, and professional-level athletes are all measured in the 40-yard dash. Theoretically, the 40 can be correlated to the ability to play. To a certain extent, this correlation is real, but not necessarily at higher levels of competition.

In recent history and at the lower levels of competition, the importance placed on the 40 has been accentuated, partly due to the attention the mass media has placed on measuring the 40. Additionally, during the NFL draft the 40 is a measurement that the general public can quickly relate to and many viewers have some limited understanding of what a good time might be. This chapter briefly covers why the 40 is used in athletics, what sports the 40 is appropriate for, and how the 40 is measured.

Why Is the 40 Used in Athletics?

Several reasons exist to measure the 40. Most obviously, it is a quick measure of speed. It also determines the ability to start, accelerate from a complete stop, reach maximal speed, and maintain that speed. Fortunately, all of these aspects can be trained.

The 40 is an easy test to administer. It can be set up nearly anywhere with a good sprinting surface. Ideally, the surface would be consistent and in a controlled environment, because varying surfaces and weather conditions can significantly affect times. Generally speaking, the difficulty of set-up and testing is minimal.

In most cases, times can also be compared from place to place and between athletes. However, several techniques may be used to intentionally reduce the times, including shortening the distance, running on a slight downhill, using track shoes, and running on a track surface. These things are done to draw attention to the athlete or team. The media picks up on the how fast the team or individual is, which often has an effect on the competition or on the marketing of the team or athlete.

The 40 can be used as an indicator of fitness. If an athlete can keep his body-fat percentage down, he is more likely to run a better time. In most cases, keeping body fat low is desirable and is associated with high fitness levels.

The 40 can also be used to compare times from year to year. For instance, an athlete's time can be compared to previous performances to determine if he is improving or not.

For Which Sports Is the 40 Important?

The measurement of the 40 is most appropriate for ground-based, strength-power sports in which running and accelerating are important. These sports include football, baseball, soccer, basketball, track, and rugby, to name just a few. It should be noted that the most important factors that contribute to sport performance are sport-specific skills. It does not matter if an athlete can run a fast 40-yard time for football if he cannot block, catch, throw, run, or tackle. However, all other things being equal (i.e., given two athletes who can block, catch, throw, or tackle equally well), coaches may assume that the faster athlete will be more successful.

How Is the 40 Measured?

The 40 is most often measured using a hand-held stopwatch, which is perhaps the most inexpensive and practical method (Figure 1-1). To measure the 40 this way, the timer stands at the end of the course and waits to see the first movement of the runner, at which point he starts the watch. When the athlete crosses the finish line, the watch is stopped (Figure 1-2).

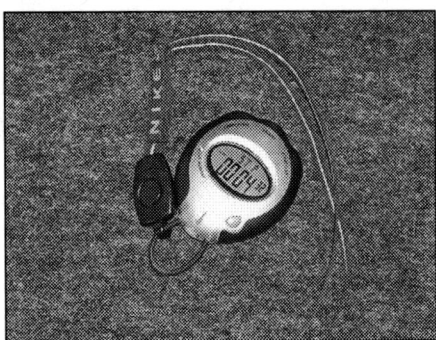

Figure 1-1. Stopwatch

Figure 1-2. The coach stops the watch when the athlete crosses the finish line.

The disadvantage to this method is that the timer's reaction time is included in the actual running time. In other words, the timer could anticipate the athlete's start, making the athlete seem slower (i.e., the watch starts before the athlete moves). The timer could also react slowly to the athlete's start, making the athlete seem faster (i.e., the watch starts after the athlete moves). This human error effectively makes all hand-held 40 times inherently inaccurate. This inaccuracy is not a problem as long as hand-held times are only compared to other hand-held times. Another problem with hand-held times is that the timer often misses the start of the athlete. If the timer misses, or slightly delays starting the watch, it results in additional inaccuracies.

Several different devices can be used to more accurately measure the time, including electronic devices that use infrared light to activate the clock (Figure 1-3). Used properly, these devices offer some advantages, including reliability. A drawback is that if the athlete started behind the first electronic gate, he would have the advantage of gaining momentum before the time actually starts.

Pressure plates can be used as well. The athlete places a hand on the pressure plate and when the hand is lifted off the plate the time starts. Athletes will often "roll

Figure 1-3. Electronic timing device

the start" by leaving the hand on the plate while the body moves forward. This technique makes this method inaccurate and inconsistent.

A combination of electronic and hand-held methods can also be used. For instance, a person can activate an electronic timer, while an infrared light stops the timer at the completion of the run. This combination may appear odd, but the authors have observed this method while testing professional football players.

Video recording of the 40 is another option for measuring. Some digital software is commercially available that can be used for this purpose, but it is impractical for most situations due to cost.

What Are Good Times in the 40?

Good times depend on the level of competition and the position played. Clearly, a lineman is going to run more slowly than a receiver. And a college player will run faster than a junior high player. Figure 1-4 provides examples of 40 times for football at various levels of competition.

High School	Below Average	Average	Above Average
Offensive/Defensive Lineman	Greater than 5.6	5.4–5.6	Less than 5.3
Tight Ends/Full Backs/Linebackers	Greater than 5.4	5.1–5.3	Less than 5.1
Halfbacks/Receivers/Defensive Backs	Greater than 5.0	4.8–5.0	Less than 4.8

College	Below Average	Average	Above Average
Offensive/Defensive Lineman	Greater than 5.1	5.1–5.3	Less than 5.3
Tight Ends/Full Backs/Linebackers	Greater than 4.9	4.8–4.9	Less than 4.8
Halfbacks, Receivers/Defensive Backs	Greater than 4.7	4.5–4.7	Less than 4.5

Professional	Below Average	Average	Above Average
Offensive/Defensive Lineman	Greater than 4.9	4.7–4.9	Less than 4.7
Tight Ends/Full Backs/Linebackers	Greater than 4.7	4.5–4.7	Less than 4.5
Halfbacks/Receivers/Defensive Backs	Greater than 4.6	4.4–4.5	Less than 4.4

Figure 1-4. Categorization of 40 times for football players at various levels of competition

When it comes to measuring the 40, it's important to understand that several methods can be used. Each has advantages (e.g., more accurate, less expensive, easier to set up), but each also has drawbacks (e.g., cost, reaction time of the timer). Each method can also be cheated. It is important for a coach to understand these methods and to select the one that is best for his team's situation. It's also important to understand that for the times to be comparable between athletes and between seasons, the same methods must be used each time.

2

Before Starting a Conditioning Program

As always, the primary concern while training is safety. Inherent risks exist while exercising, but a coach's ultimate goal is to keep the risk of training to a minimum, which can be accomplished in several different ways.

Before training, the surrounding area should be checked for such things as surface condition, broken glass, uneven surfaces, and obstructions that would limit the space in which the athletes can move. Generally speaking, adequate space must be available in all directions. Training for speed requires top speeds, explosive starts, and an adequate deceleration zone. The surface should preferably be dry, flat, fairly short, and on natural grass. A good pair of cleats should be used as well, which will limit the risk of slipping.

Several good training practices will maximize the training effect. A comprehensive warm-up time should be allotted. The warm-up should be gradual, dynamic, and specific in nature, and should include some light jogging and low-level hops, skips, and bounds in all directions integrated with dynamic stretching. Several progressive speed sprints finish the warm-up before the training session begins. The warm-up will be covered in more detail in Chapter 9.

Training alone can be problematic if an athlete is at risk for injury. Therefore, it is recommended that athletes train in pairs or groups. Everyone present should know the address of where they are in case of emergency. A phone should also be available, as well as a vehicle for transportation if necessary.

Get a Doctor's Clearance to Participate

Any time an individual begins an athletic or conditioning program, it's important that he first gets a doctor's clearance to participate. While many athletes will assume that they are in good enough shape to begin a new program, a condition or injury may exist that could become very serious as a result of participation. A doctor's clearance is especially important if the athlete is just starting out, or if he has been away from athletics and training for an extended period.

The doctor will be looking for any medical condition that may jeopardize that athlete's health, including orthopedic dysfunctions and systemic issues such as asthma, cardiac function, or any pre-existing conditioning that could predispose the athlete to health risks. As a coach, your full cooperation with the medical staff is mandatory.

Understand the Difference Between Soreness and Injury

Hard training will make anyone sore, as will injuries. Sometimes it's difficult for athletes to distinguish between being sore and being injured. Consider the following general guidelines to help you determine the difference between soreness and injury:

- Normal soreness should go away in one to three days. If the soreness lingers, it may be something more serious.
- Normal soreness should be located in the muscles, not in the joints. Pain in an athlete's knee, ankle, or other joint is not a normal response to training and should be taken seriously.

If an athlete is sore from a hard workout, several things can be done to help. First, the athlete should consider icing the sore muscles following the training session and again at night. Second, he should apply massage to the affected muscles. Third, he should get some rest. It is not smart to exercise a muscle when it is very sore.

If a pain is more serious than soreness, several things should be done. First, stop the activity that is causing the injury. Second, have the athlete apply ice to the area often throughout the day. Third, have the athlete go see a doctor and follow his or her advice. Ignoring small injuries tends to make them turn into big ones.

Quick Tip for Athletes

Don't ignore injuries. It only tends to make them worse.

Start Slowly

The need to start slowly is mentioned repeatedly throughout this book, and for good reason. It is important for an athlete to first learn the skills and then build up the fitness base slowly over time. Failure to do so will mean that an athlete will not have the skills or fitness level needed for the advanced drills and workouts still to come. In the long run, progressing too quickly will result in wasted time and possible injury. Instead, athletes must learn the basic skills until they can do them correctly without having to think about them. Athletes should perform the beginning workouts to build their fitness level, then move to the next level. Don't make the mistake of starting your athletes' workouts at too high a level in terms of difficulty and fitness.

Quick Tip for Athletes

Don't just open up the book and begin with the world class program.
Take the time to master the skills and get in shape.

Be Ready for the Weather

Weather is a major cause of injury in athletics, so be prepared for it. This chapter addresses the two extremes—heat and cold.

Training outside in the hot weather can cause a lot of problems for an athlete, up to and including death. Have your athletes adhere to the following guidelines for hot-weather training:

- Acclimatize: Going from an air-conditioned environment to hard training in the heat can be a huge jolt to the body, so it's important for athletes to get used to the heat gradually. Ideally, the full workout should be phased in over several weeks. For example, first the warm-up is performed outside, then both the warm-up and the cool-down, and then the entire workout. This technique gives the body a chance to get used to training in the heat.

- Wear sunscreen: Direct exposure to the sun is dangerous. Direct sun can cause sunburns, which can incapacitate an athlete, and it can also increase the risk of developing skin cancer. Athletes should wear sunscreen when training outside to protect themselves from the sun's harmful effects.

- Utilize the shade: Have shade available if athletes are training in hot and/or humid conditions. Shade will give the athletes a place to get some relief from the sun and the heat.

- Wear light-colored clothing: Light-colored clothing will help reflect heat and protect athletes from becoming overheated.

- Wear clothes that breathe: Doing so will allow the athlete to perspire. If an athlete cannot perspire adequately, he may overheat, which could lead to a very dangerous situation.
- Drink water: When athletes train outside, they sweat. Staying hydrated helps keep athletes from overheating. If they don't replace fluids lost through sweat, they become very prone to overheating. It is essential that athletes drink water constantly—throughout the day before training, right before the training session, every 10 to 20 minutes during training, and throughout the day after training.

Training outside in cold weather is also important, because many sports are played outside in the winter. Adhere to the following guidelines for cold-weather training:

- Acclimatize: Just like with hot environments, it's important for athletes to gradually get used to cold weather.
- Dress in layers: Even if it is cold outside, exercise is going to warm up the body. Dressing in layers is important, because as athletes get warmed up, they are going to want to remove layers of clothing so that they do not become too hot. It's better to wear several layers of clothing that can be removed than one heavy item.
- Drink water: Even though it's cold, athletes can still become dehydrated. Athletes should still drink water before, during, and after training.
- Warm up thoroughly: Warming up is important for preventing injuries and getting ready for work. In a cold environment, it becomes even more important for preventing injuries. Plan on increasing the time athletes spend warming up by at least 50 percent in a cold environment. They should keep warming up until they feel ready to start training.
- Keep moving: In a normal environment, athletes may stand or sit (or lie down) between sprints. Doing so is not a good idea in a cold environment because the combination of the lack of motion and sweating will cool the body down. Athletes must keep moving between exercises and, if necessary, put more clothes on between exercises to help keep themselves warm and ready to go.

Quick Tip for Athletes

Drink water before, during, and after training,
regardless of the temperature outside.

Eat Something

Athletes need adequate fuel to have a good training session, and they must have a good training session to get good results. They cannot skip meals and expect to perform well—they need that food for fuel. Preferably, athletes should eat a light meal 30 to 90 minutes before training, and have plenty of water as well. This intake will minimize metabolic stress and cap off energy stores before training. Additionally, eating a simple carbohydrate and protein snack (e.g., a piece of fruit and a glass of milk) immediately after training will speed recovery. Eating a meal within two hours of training will help replenish the energy stores.

Quick Tip for Athletes

> Eat a light meal 30 to 90 minutes before training
> and another immediately after the workout.

Taking a few simple precautions can make the difference between having a good training experience and having a disastrous one. If athletes adhere to the guidelines presented in this chapter, they will have a much better chance of having a positive training experience.

3

How Everything Works

This chapter provides an overview of the science behind training for the 40. It's important to understand this information so that you can develop a safe, effective running technique and training program. Failing to understand these concepts can result in athletes adopting unsafe, ineffective training, falling prey to gimmicks, or just wasting time.

Why Do People Move the Way They Do?

Structure and Function

Skeletal muscles attach to bones via tendons. Skeletal muscles are organized into layers of bundles made up of smaller fibers. At the biggest level are bundles of muscle fibers (which are the functional units of the muscles). Individual muscle fibers are themselves composed of bundles of smaller myofibrils, which contain myofilaments. The myofilaments are what make the muscles shorten and therefore allow people to move.

Muscular Contractions

When running the 40, two types of muscular contractions come into play—isometric and isotonic. Isometric contractions occur when the force exerted by the muscles is equal to the resistance. In other words, the muscle doesn't change length. While such contractions never truly take place outside of specifically designed machines, times arise when athletes get close to performing a true isometric contraction. For example, if an athlete is performing a heavy bench press and the weight gets stuck a few inches off of his chest, then he will perform an isometric contraction until his muscles get too tired to fight the weight. In sprinting, when the foot strikes the ground, the runner wants to maintain his posture at footstrike (i.e., knees should not flex, hips should not sag, etc.), which is close to an isometric contraction.

An isotonic contraction occurs when the muscle changes length. Isotonic contractions are categorized as either concentric or eccentric. A concentric contraction occurs when the muscle shortens (i.e., applied force is sufficient to overcome the resistance). Holding a dumbbell in one hand and curling it to the shoulder is an example of a concentric contraction. An eccentric contraction occurs when the muscle lengthens (i.e., the force applied is less than the resistance). Lowering the dumbbell from the shoulder back to the side involves an eccentric contraction of the biceps.

Elastic Energy

Understanding the different contraction types is important when designing exercises to improve athletic performance. A fast eccentric contraction followed immediately by a fast concentric contraction generates more force than normal—the result of elastic energy. Individuals competing in almost every event in athletics would benefit from tapping into this elastic energy. The foot-strike while sprinting is an example of using elastic energy. When a runner drives the foot toward the ground, the quadriceps are lengthening (eccentric contraction). When the foot strikes the ground, runners keep the thigh, shin, and ankle tense (almost an isometric contraction). This tension is important to keep elastic energy from dissipating at the footstrike. They then pull and push themselves forward using the elastic energy that was generated by the footstrike.

Terminology

Certain terminology is necessary to fully understand a discussion of speed training:

- *Velocity*—how quickly someone moves from point A to point B
- *Acceleration*—a positive change in velocity (i.e., an increase in how fast someone is running)
- *Deceleration*—a negative change in velocity (i.e., a decrease in how fast someone is running)

Newton's Laws of Motion

Isaac Newton formulated three laws of motion that are important in sprinting. The information covered by Newton's laws explains a lot of the techniques involved in running the 40—from starting explosively and accelerating over the first few steps to running at maximum velocity. These laws are as follows:

- Law of inertia
- Law of acceleration
- Law of action/reaction

The law of inertia states that it takes a force to start, stop, or alter motion. *Inertia* refers to an object's resistance to a change in its motion and is related to the amount of matter in an object (i.e., the more mass in the object, the more inertia it has) and to where that mass is located. For example, when sprinting at maximum velocity, athletes should bring the heel up to the hip before lifting the knee in front. This technique keeps the mass of the leg near the hip, which allows the limb to be moved more quickly.

The law of acceleration states that the rate of change in an object's motion is proportionate to the amount of force applied and the direction in which that force is applied. The equation "force equals mass times acceleration" stems from this law, which implies that it takes great strength to move fast, as that force must be directed against the ground to help change a person's motion.

The law of action/reaction states that for every action, an equal and opposite reaction takes place. As a runner directs force into the ground from a powerful footstrike, the ground directs force back up into the runner.

Why Do Athletes Train the Way They Do?

It is important thing to remember that some people are just naturally fast. If someone is not naturally fast, he can improve through very hard training, but he is not going to have the same ultimate potential as someone naturally gifted with speed. The following three characteristic contribute to natural speed:

- Makeup of the muscles
- How muscles are shaped
- Innate explosiveness

Makeup of the Muscles

Muscles are made up of muscle fibers, which are the functional units of the muscles. Muscle fibers can run the entire length of the muscle and are grouped together into motor units, which in turn consist of the motor nerve that leaves the spinal cord and all of the muscle fibers for which it is responsible. Some motor units have few muscle fibers (e.g., those responsible for gross actions like walking), while others have a lot of muscle fibers (e.g., those responsible for the fine control, such as the eye muscles). Motor nerves deliver messages from the brain and spinal cord that tell the body to move.

Several types of muscle fibers exist. Everyone is born with a certain percentage of each type, and the breakdown helps to determine ultimate potential. The types of muscle fibers are as follows:

- *Slow-twitch*—Slow-twitch fibers are resistant to fatigue. They are developed primarily through aerobic exercise. They generate very little force (compared to the fast-twitch fibers) and do so very slowly.
- *Fast-twitch, fatigue resistant*—These fibers generate more force than slow-twitch fibers, do so faster than slow-twitch fibers, and are also resistant to fatigue. They are developed through longer sprints (200 and 400 meters), or weight training with moderate-to-high volumes (more than eight repetitions).
- *Fast-twitch, fatigable*—These fibers generate the most force of all three fiber types and generate force the fastest, but they also fatigue the fastest. Short sprints, plyometrics, and heavy weight training are all examples of activities that develop fast-twitch, fatigable fibers.

Other fiber types exist that are basically hybrids of the three previously listed. In other words, other fiber types may include one with mostly slow characteristics and some fast-twitch, fatigue-resistant characteristics.

Most people are born with 50 percent slow-twitch fibers and 50 percent fast-twitch fibers. Clearly, the more fast-twitch muscle fibers a person has, the better his potential for being fast and explosive. Unfortunately, the percentage of fast-twitch fibers cannot be increased through training; athletes can only develop what they have. If a person has only 20 percent fast-twitch muscle fibers, he has very little potential, no matter his level of enthusiasm.

How Muscles Are Shaped

All muscle fibers run in a certain direction. Some run straight up and down, while others run at an angle. If they run at an angle, they have better potential to exert force. However, if the fibers run straight up and down, they can shorten more quickly and help an athlete run faster.

It is unclear whether people have any control over the direction in which the fibers run. It appears that with a lot of bodybuilding-type training people can increase the angle at which the fibers run. But it is unclear if people can make the fibers run straight up and down as a result of training. In other words, training like a bodybuilder can potentially negatively impact the ability to run faster, but it is unclear if making the fibers run up and down is genetic or trainable.

Some evidence shows that how muscle mass is distributed can impact speed. Having more muscle mass on the upper part of the thighs and hamstrings seems to result in faster speeds than having the muscle mass distributed throughout the thighs and hamstrings. Unfortunately, this factor is most likely genetic.

Innate Explosiveness

Explosiveness is an ill-defined quality, though everyone knows it when they see it. Some people are just wired to be fast and explosive. Many reasons may exist to explain this added explosiveness—muscle fiber type, muscle shape, how nerves control the muscle fibers, ability to recruit fibers quickly, psychological focus, etc.

It's important to understand why some people are faster than others. This knowledge is used later in this book to help explain how and why the training programs are being developed. Two key points are that adequate fuel must be present to allow an athlete to be fast, and that athletes must avoid things that will interfere with their speed.

Adequate Fuel

Athletes must have enough fuel to be able to perform. Eating right is essential, but the ability to utilize fuels can be developed through training. Stated simply, the body uses three energy systems to fuel performance:

- Phosphagen system
- Glycolytic system
- Aerobic system

The phosphagen system fuels exercise for approximately six to 10 seconds. Exercise can be so sudden and so intense that athletes cannot use oxygen to help break down fuel. This system relies on fuel that is stored in the muscles as *adenosine triphosphate* (ATP). Only a finite amount of ATP can be stored in the muscles, usually only enough for the first few seconds of movement. After that, athletes begin to resynthesize ATP from a product called *creatine phosphate* (CP). Ultimately, this energy system (and performance of short-term activities) is limited by the amounts of ATP and CP stored in the muscles. The phosphagen system fuels short-term, high-intensity exercise such as performing a vertical jump, throwing a shot put, or running the 40.

The glycolytic system provides fuel for up to two to three minutes, though the exercise is not as highly intense as that seen with the phosphagen system. The glycolytic system relies upon glycogen stored in the muscles and liver (i.e., stored carbohydrates). It takes longer to break down glycogen, which is why the intensity level in this energy system is not as high as in the phosphagen system. This energy system also produces a waste product called lactic acid, which causes the burning sensation in the muscles during exercise. Eventually, lactic acid interferes with the ability of muscles to contract, which of course interferes with performance. Activities that last up to two to three minutes—including running 200 to 400 meters or performing sit-ups or push-ups for two minutes—would be fueled by the glycolytic energy system.

The aerobic energy system fuels exercise as long as fuel remains available, but does so slowly and at a very low intensity. The aerobic energy system also relies upon glycogen for fuel, but also uses fat and, in extreme cases, even protein as fuel sources. This energy system requires very-low-intensity activity, because enough oxygen must be available to assist with breaking down fat for fuel. If sufficient oxygen is not available, then the athlete is using one of the other two energy systems. The drawback is that using oxygen to help break down fuel is a slow process, which is why people cannot run a mile at the same pace with which they run the 40. The good news is that as long as fuel is available, and as long as the intensity is relatively low, this system can fuel exercise almost indefinitely.

Conditioning programs can be designed to address muscle shape and fuel availability. For example, if an athlete knows that he wants to target his fast-twitch muscle fibers, he would perform short-duration, explosive exercises. Likewise, to improve the phosphagen energy system's ability to contribute to performance, he'd need to focus on short-duration, high-intensity exercises that allow for full recovery. Running four or five miles a day, while great for the aerobic energy system, will not contribute to performance on the 40. In fact, running four or five miles a day may actually interfere with performance on the 40.

Don't Interfere With Speed

Only a limited amount of time is available each day to devote to training, which means that coaches want training sessions to be safe and effective. One of the ways to be sure that training is effective is to avoid those activities that will interfere with speed development, such as the following:

- Overdeveloping slow-twitch muscle fibers
- Performing too much bodybuilding-type training
- Overdeveloping the aerobic energy system

Focusing on endurance work (i.e., long-duration activities with short recovery periods) is a great way to develop those slow-twitch muscle fibers. The problem is that this type of training will cause the fast-twitch muscle fibers to take on slow characteristics, which is counterproductive when the goal is a faster 40. Therefore, training needs to focus on speed and explosiveness. To be faster, an athlete needs to eat, sleep, and live speed.

Bodybuilding training is defined as training that focuses on moderate volumes (generally eight to 15 repetitions), at moderate intensities (as much weight as the athlete can lift eight to 15 times), with short recoveries (generally about 30 to 60 seconds per set). Exercises are focused on body parts as opposed to movements. Bodybuilding training is great for fitness and appearance. However, a danger exists that too much of this type of training can reorient the muscle fibers so that their velocity of shortening decreases. The strength-training programs presented in this book focus on three things: preventing injuries, improving the ability to exert force against the ground, and improving explosiveness.

Finally, the aerobic energy system is important for fitness, but overdeveloping it will interfere with speed on the 40 for a number of reasons. First, it will mean that the athlete's training is focused on developing the slow-twitch muscle fibers. Second, aerobic training involves running slowly for long periods of time, which means that the athlete is not learning to become fast for a short period of time. Third, aerobic training develops the wrong energy system, and time would be better spent developing the phosphagen energy system.

Quick Tip for Athletes

> To improve speed, training needs to focus on the right muscle fibers and the right energy system.

How Do Athletes Learn to Run Fast?

According to research, agility, the ability to run at top speed, and acceleration are generally unrelated to each other. Most coaches have observed these qualities in their athletes. One athlete will be able to run in a straight line quite well, but not be able to change direction. Another athlete will be explosive off the line, but have no real top-end speed. As a coach, you will have to determine what the needs of your athletes are and prioritize the training schedule. Fortunately, agility, top speed, and acceleration are trainable and an individual approach can be used.

Motor learning is the study of how people learn to move. At certain times during physical development, athletes have windows of opportunity where motor learning is optimized. No matter how old an athlete is, he can always learn new motor patterns. Ideally, coaches will initially teach them correct movement. Therefore, they will not develop bad habits or have to relearn correct technique.

Quick Tip for Athletes

> Immediately correct any movement errors or bad habits. Continuing to reinforce bad movement techniques is extremely counterproductive.

Running the 40 is what is called a *"closed skill,"* which means that the athlete knows what needs to be completed and no adjustments need to be made during the action. The 40 can be broken down and taught in progressive sequences from the start, through the acceleration, to top speed. Two concepts are important for understanding how people learn to be fast: sequential dependency and automation.

Sequential Dependency

The final outcome of a movement is dependant on the preceding actions. For example, to complete a successful lay-up, a basketball player would need to coordinate the approach while dribbling, stop dribbling, take off from one foot, and hit the right location on the backboard with the ball. To a certain extent, the same thing can be said for the 40. A proper starting position will ensure acceleration potential. Once top speed is reached, it will need to be maintained.

Automation

An athlete should continue to perform every movement until it becomes automated. For example, children who are learning to tie their shoes do not have the coordination of the motor pattern until it is repeated many times. As adults, the motor pattern is automated, meaning that adults don't need to think about the action and instead "call up" and execute the motor pattern. Proper execution of the start, the acceleration, and maintenance of top speed are skills that can become, to a degree, automated.

This model of the learning sequences could be used to help an athlete learn to run a fast 40:

- Begin by getting the athlete comfortable with a proper starting position. The athlete will develop strength in this position over time. It is important not to vary the starting position on a day-to-day basis, which would fail to reinforce a strong motor pattern or maximize starting ability. The starting position is described in Chapter 4. Maximal acceleration potential cannot be achieved if the athlete is not in a proper starting position.

- Once the athlete is familiar with the starting position, he should learn to sequence his upper- and lower-body movements. This sequence may or may not come naturally, so it may be necessary to perform the first few steps slowly. Again, it is optimal to reinforce the same motor pattern with each repetition to maximize potential.

- Running at top speed can be approached with different tactics, including always starting before building up to top speed. Another tactic is to slowly accelerate to top speed and then focus on maintaining that top speed. In either case, proper form at top speed is critical. Biomechanical analysis of top speed is provided in Chapter 6.

Quick Tip for Athletes

The saying, "Perfect practice makes perfect" is absolutely true. Maximize training time and adaptation by always focusing on proper technique.

Part II: Application

4

The Start Position

The start of the 40 is the most critical aspect of achieving a good time. The majority of athletes either do not know how to start or how to focus enough training on the start—or both. Observing starting technique at the high school level will reveal everything from a four-point defensive lineman's goal-line technique to a two-point position with the shoulders perpendicular to the starting line.

Properly adjusting the starting position can cut as much as two tenths of a second off the overall time. This chapter presents a step-by-step procedure for assuming the starting position.

Consider that the timer should be standing at the end of the 40. The timer will begin his watch on the athlete's first movement. Since the average human reaction time is 0.24 seconds, the athlete should try to move from the start as quickly as possible so that he can cover more ground before the timer can react and begin the watch. Covering maximum distance is predicated on a sound starting position. At the end of the 40, the timer will always stop the watch at the appropriate time because it is easy to watch the athlete run and anticipate when he will cross the finish line, which will negate any reaction time advantages at the end of the sprint. Because the beginning of the sprint is the only chance the athlete has to take advantage of the timer's slow reaction time, a solid starting position is critical to performance.

Keep the following in mind when working on developing a proper starting position:

- Athletes and coaches should not have a "special" starting technique. It is most efficient to use the one described in this chapter and focus on getting comfortable with the technique. Anything else will reduce performance.
- Coaches should only allow athletes to practice running the 40 from a three-point start, because that is the standard starting position used during testing.

- Using proper starting technique is the best way to immediately run a faster 40.
- Cleats are critical for the 40. Athletes must wear them at all times while training during the weeks before the season.

Starting Stance Procedure

Step 1 (Figure 4-1)—Place the toes of the rear foot exactly one shoe length behind the starting line.

Figure 4-1

Step 2 (Figure 4-2)—Place the opposite toes at the heels of the front foot.

Figure 4-2

Step 3 (Figure 4-3)—Maintain hip distance from side to side.

Figure 4-3

Step 4 (Figure 4-4)—If the left foot is forward, the right hand will be right behind the starting line.

Figure 4-4

Step 5—Raise the hips above shoulder level.

Step 6—Bend the elbow of the left arm to 90 degrees and raise the arm to full extension (assuming the right foot is forward).

Step 7—Tuck the head slightly downward.

Step 8 (Figure 4-5)—Balance the body weight between the front and rear foot.

Figure 4-5

Quick Tip for Athletes

Keep the rear elbow bent at 90 degrees. It can be brought through more quickly from this position, because the center of gravity is close to the axis of rotation/shoulder joint. Also, it is an easy cue for the timer to focus on if your hand is up.

5

Acceleration

The acceleration phase is the period from the first movement out of the starting position until the athlete reaches top speed. Depending on the athlete, it may take 20 yards to hit top speed or he may actually still be accelerating at the end of the 40.

Keep a few key elements of the acceleration in mind while training:

- The acceleration phase is critical to running the best time.
- The starting stance will predetermine how effectively an athlete transitions into the acceleration phase.
- If running mechanics are lost during the acceleration phase, it is nearly impossible to effectively run at top speed.

The acceleration phase can be broken down into two subphases, the initial drive phase and the subsequent acceleration. Each of these phases is discussed in detail in the following sections.

Drive Phase

The drive phase is the period from the starting position to when the athlete begins to use what are termed the "backside mechanics" of running. Frontside mechanics involve all action that takes place in front of the body. The drive phase involves nearly 100 percent frontside mechanics. Several key elements of the drive phase should be addressed at all times during training. Figure 5-1 lists common errors made during the drive phase as well as appropriate corrections.

- Stay low: Nearly all inexperienced athletes run too high too early. It takes time to develop the ability to stay low during this phase. Staying low places the body in a better position to apply more force longer than when standing up, which translates to a better time.

- Tuck the head: Athletes must keep the head slightly tucked and the eyes focused down. This position ensures that the athlete will stay low in the drive phase and keep the hips in a better position to push.
- Actions should be forward and back, not side to side: Side-to-side motion is a huge waste of time when running the 40. Athletes must focus on forward and backward movements, including movement of the knees, foot placement, hand action, elbow movement, etc.
- Push, don't pull, through this phase: The large hip muscles are by far the body's strongest. Starting low and staying low will ensure that the athlete pushes out of the starting stance and activates these muscles. If an athlete reaches out with each step and begins to stand up too early, it will sacrifice the efficiency of the movement in the drive phase.

Common Drive Phase Errors	Corrections
Standing up too early	Focus on pushing the feet. Keep the head in a neutral position or even tucked and not look at the finish.
Overstriding	Focus on quick feet and staying low. Keep the eyes focused about three to five yards in front.
Lateral movement of the arms	Keep the elbows close to the body and the elbows flexed as close to 90 degrees as possible.

Figure 5-1. Common drive phase errors and appropriate corrections

Acceleration Phase

The acceleration phase is the period from the end of the drive phase to when the athlete begins running at top speed. Several key elements of the acceleration phase should be addressed at all times during training. Figure 5-2 lists common errors made during the acceleration phase as well as appropriate corrections.

- Stay low: Nearly all inexperienced athletes run too high too early. It takes time to develop the ability to stay low during this phase.
- Use proper foot placement: Taking strides that are too long can slow down an athlete's run. "Overstriding" can cause an athlete to brake with every step, thereby slowing him down. An athlete will know that he is overstriding if he finds himself leaning backward as he takes each step.
- Actions should be forward and back, not side to side: as in the drive phase, the athlete must focus on forward and backward movements.

Common Acceleration Phase Errors	Corrections
Standing up too early	Focus on pushing, or pounding the feet. Keep the head in a neutral position and not look at the finish.
Overstriding	Focus on quick feet and staying low. Keep the eyes focused about 10 yards in front.
Lateral movement of the arms	Keep the elbows close to the body and the elbows flexed as close to 90 degrees as possible.
Foot placement that is too wide	Lift the knees directly up and cast the foot (refer to Chapter 6).

Figure 5-2. Common acceleration phase errors and appropriate corrections

It is critical that every athlete masters the acceleration phase, which transitions the runner from the drive phase to top speed. Keeping proper mechanics during this phase will ensure that an athlete achieves his best time. Lack of proper mechanics during the acceleration phase can add a significant amount of time to performance of the 40.

6

Top Speed

During the first 10 to 20 yards of acceleration, the athlete should be transitioning into top-speed running form. Top-speed running is different from the acceleration phase in that the athlete is concerned with leg motion both behind and in front of the body. During the acceleration phase, the leg motion is predominately coming from the front of the body.

The sprinting motion can be divided into two phases: takeoff and footstrike. This chapter provides a discussion of technique during those phases, as well as of other aspects of the top-speed phase, such as arm motion, what to do with the rest of the upper body, and finishing the sprint.

Takeoff

After the foot has struck the ground, the athlete should begin pulling himself over the foot. As his hips move forward, he will shift to having just the ball of the foot on the ground (Figure 6-1). As the hips continue to move forward, the foot will break contact with the ground.

When the foot breaks contact with the ground, the athlete lifts up the big toe and tries to keep his foot rigid. The ankle should be at roughly a 90-degree angle. This technique is called "casting" the foot (Figure 6-2).

Quick Tip for Athletes

Casting of the foot allows maximum speed to occur.

Figure 6-1

Figure 6-2

After the foot leaves the ground and is cast, the athlete brings his heel straight up toward the hip. If this technique is done correctly, the knee should travel forward somewhat. Have the athlete think of sliding his heel against an imaginary wall behind him. This technique "shortens the lever," which means that by bringing the heel to the hip, the athlete will reduce the angular momentum, thereby allowing him to eventually swing the leg more quickly. As he brings his heel to his hip, the athlete must remember to keep the ankle cast (Figure 6-3).

Once the heel reaches the hip, the athlete must lift his knee up. Cue the athlete at this point to think about stepping over the opposite knee, which gives him a guide regarding how high to lift the knee. As he is lifting the knee, he must remember to keep his ankle cast. When the knee lifts up, the leg will automatically unfold; it's not something he will have to think about (Figure 6-4). From that position, the athlete drives his foot down to the ground from the hips.

Figure 6-3

Figure 6-4

Quick Tip for Athletes

> To improve your mechanics, try to bring your heel to your hip and step over the opposite knee.

Footstrike

The foot should strike the ground slightly in front of the hips (Figure 6-5). Striking too far in front of the hips (i.e., overstriding) will result in braking, which will slow the runner down. One way to know if an athlete is overstriding is that you will see him leaning backward while running (Figure 6-6).

Figure 6-5

Figure 6-6

When the foot strikes the ground, the foot should still be cast (i.e., it should still be rigid). The athlete must keep the big toe pulled up and strike the ground with the ball of the foot. He must avoid running heel-to-toe. This error is covered in more detail in Chapter 13.

As the foot strikes the ground, the athlete should concentrate on keeping the torso and leg rigid. He must avoid sinking into his leg or letting his hips sink down, both of which will dissipate that elastic energy that he's worked so hard to generate.

Quick Tip for Athletes

> When running at top speed, land on the ball of your foot and drive the foot down using your glutes.

Swinging the Arms

The arm swing plays an important role in running fast. The arms act in opposition to the legs, help the runner maintain balance, and help him maintain running efficiency. The athlete should concentrate on driving his arms back hard. If this happens, a reflex will kick in at the shoulder that will move the arm forward automatically; the athlete won't have to think about it. The arms should remain tight to the body and be pumped forward and backward (Figure 6-7). The athlete must not allow the arms to fly away from the body or cross the midline (also known as "running like a chicken") (Figure 6-8). Running like a chicken will cause the body to rotate while running, which will negatively impact speed.

Figure 6-7

Figure 6-8

The Rest of the Upper Body

After the first 20 yards or so, the athlete should focus on running tall, which means avoiding leaning forward, looking down, and slouching. Leaning forward will result in the athlete having less range of motion at the hips, so he will not be able to exert as much force into the ground during the sprint. Looking down and slouching will result in the leaning forward.

Teach the athletes to focus on looking ahead. They must also keep the shoulders back and the chest out. They should run with the upper body relaxed, because tension will affect an athlete's speed.

Finishing the Sprint

The following point cannot be emphasized enough: The athlete must not slow down until he's run across the finish line. Many athletes begin slowing down in anticipation before they reach the finish line, which means that their 40 time will be slower than it should be. Teach them to focus on a point beyond the finish line and run to the point.

Following are summaries of the major cues for each phase of running at top speed. The common errors and corrections for each phase are listed in Figures 6-9 through 6-12. Note that many of the remedial drills are described in Chapter 9.

Takeoff Phase Cues

- Pull the hips over the foot.
- Push the body forward.
- Cast the foot.
- Heel to hip.
- Step over the opposite knee.
- Drive the foot down using the glute.

Footstrike Cues

- Keep the foot cast.
- Land on the ball of the foot.
- Keep the leg and torso rigid.

Common Takeoff Phase Errors	Correction:
The foot is not cast, which results in possible injury and dissipation of elastic energy at the footstrike.	Pay attention to casting the foot. Perform remedial ankling drills to reinforce.
The knee points down when the heel is brought to the hip, which will take longer to cycle the leg forward, slowing the runner down.	Focus on trying to slide the heel up against an imaginary wall behind him. Perform remedial butt-kick drills.
The knee is brought up too soon, which means that the heel will not be in contact with the hip, increasing the angular momentum when cycling the leg forward and slowing the runner down.	Focus on trying to slide the heel up against an imaginary wall behind him. Perform remedial butt-kick drills.
Failure to step over opposite knee, which means that the knee is not being brought high enough, reducing how much force the runner can exert into the ground and slowing him down.	Perform remedial high knee drills to reinforce how high the knee should be lifted.
Using the quadriceps to drive the foot down, which results in less force being exerted into the ground, slowing the runner down.	Perform remedial A and B drills to reinforce how to use the hips to make contact with the ground.

Figure 6-9

Common Footstrike Errors	Corrections
Landing on the toes, which will cause the runner to brake, slowing him down. This error may cause or aggravate shin splints.	Focus on landing on the ball of the foot, not the toes. If necessary, perform remedial ankling drills.
Landing on the heel, which is usually part of a heel-to-toe running motion. When going from heel-to-toe, the runner will brake. Also, landing on the heel tends to overly stress the hamstrings, which is one reason why sprinters and runners get hamstring injuries.	Focus on landing on the ball of the foot, not the toes. If necessary, perform remedial ankling drills.
Letting the knee flex at footstrike, which will result in a dissipation of elastic energy, slowing the runner down.	Strength train for the lower extremity. Also, perform skips and hops to help strengthen the lower extremity.
Letting the hips sink at footstrike, which will result in a dissipation of elastic energy, slowing the runner down.	Perform strength training for the core muscles to help strengthen them. Also, perform hops, skips, and A drills.

Figure 6-10

Arm Swing Cues

- Keep arms tight to the body.
- Pump the arms forward and back.
- Drive the arms back.

Common Arm Swing Error	Correction
Letting the arms cross the midline of the body, which can result in excessive rotation, slowing the runner down.	Perform remedial arm swing drills.

Figure 6-11

Upper Body Cues

- Look straight ahead.
- Keep the shoulders back.
- Keep the upper body relaxed.

Common Upper-Body Errors	Corrections
Looking down or slouching can cause the runner to lean forward, interfering with his ability to exert force into the ground.	Focus on running tall. Perform bounds, skips, A drills, hops, etc.
Failing to run relaxed, which will cause the limbs to move more slowly, slowing the runner down.	Perform variable-speed training, such as "ins and outs."

Figure 6-12

Understanding how to run at top speed will not only help athletes run faster, but it will also help them stay healthy. Hamstring injuries and shin splints are common in people taking up sprinting, and these problems are usually preventable with conditioning and proper technique.

Part III: Training

© Gary Rothstein

7

Training Principles

A number of variables can have a major impact on the success of a training program. How you put the training program together can impact whether the athlete meets his goals, wastes his time, or gets injured. How you apply these training variables can affect an athlete's ability to practice, recover, and ultimately perform.

Training Principles

When putting together a program to improve an athlete's performance on the 40, a number of variables should be considered. Adhering to the following principles will allow athletes to make gains safely, while failing to do so can cause a program to be a waste of time, ineffective, or even dangerous.

- Athletes get what they train for.
- Coaches have to make things more difficult.
- Athletes must walk before they run.
- It's hard to make gains, but it's easy to lose them.
- Properly putting everything together is essential.

Principle #1: Athletes Get What They Train For.

This important principle of exercise states that a coach has to decide exactly what he wants from each athlete's training and then put the program together with that goal in mind. The following qualities are very important for running the 40 more quickly, meaning that any training program that is designed to improve performance on the 40 needs to address all of these qualities:

- Strength, both to exert force into the ground and to maintain posture
- Ability to move the limbs quickly
- Ability to explosively take the first step
- Well-trained fast-twitch muscle fibers
- Ability to quickly recruit fast-twitch muscle fibers
- Well-trained phosphagen energy system
- Technique to prevent injuries and increase speed

Strength

Exercises designed to increase strength in a way that will help the 40 need to be done while standing. They also need to involve exerting force against the ground, as is done while running the 40. They should also involve several joints and muscles working together, not in isolation. Exercises such as the squat and its variations, lunges, and Romanian dead lifts are excellent choices for developing strength.

Ability to Move the Limbs Quickly

This ability is the result of dynamic flexibility and good technique. Dynamic flexibility is the ability to move a limb through its entire range of motion without impedance. This lack of impedance is important because an athlete will be able to move his limbs more quickly if nothing is resisting his motion. This ability is developed through the dynamic flexibility exercises that are described in Chapter 9. Good technique, in addition to preventing injuries, teaches athletes how to move their limbs quickly. Technique is developed first with technique drills, which break the sprinting motion down into manageable parts. It is then reinforced by actually sprinting with good technique. Technique drills are provided in Chapter 10.

Ability to Explosively Take the First Step

The faster, more explosively that an athlete can take that first step, the faster he can potentially get somewhere. A number of variables should be focused upon to improve this ability. First, an athlete must learn how to perform starts explosively. Starting technique is described in Chapter 4 and drills to train for the start are described in Chapter 10. Second, an athlete must become stronger, which will allow him to exert more force against the ground, potentially improving his speed. Finally, an athlete must learn how to move explosively. This ability is enhanced through a combination of exercises designed to teach athletes how to exert a lot of force in a short period of time—namely the power clean (described in Chapter 11) and plyometric exercises (described in Chapter 12).

Well-Trained Fast-Twitch Muscle Fibers

Training the fast-twitch muscle fibers is accomplished by focusing on shorter distances, strength training, performing explosive exercises with full recovery between sets, and using lower training volumes. Remember that doing too much endurance work (e.g., running miles, performing sets of 20 or 30 repetitions) will interfere with training for the 40, as it will develop the slow-twitch muscle fibers.

Ability to Quickly Recruit Fast-Twitch Muscle Fibers

To learn how to quickly recruit fast-twitch muscle fibers, athletes must perform exercises that teach them to move explosively. Athletes must perform exercises that teach them to exert a lot of force in a short period of time.

Well-Trained Phosphagen Energy System

Chapter 3 describes the different energy systems that are used during athletic performance. Given the short, highly intense nature of the 40, the phosphagen energy system will be the predominant system for the activity, which means that athletes need to spend time developing this energy system. This training will be done through shorter sprints (up to about 60 yards), plyometrics, and low-volume weight training (up to four or five repetitions per set). Activities should have a high level of intensity (in fact, they should be "all-out" efforts), with full recovery between attempts.

Technique to Prevent Injuries and Increase Speed

Good technique accomplishes two objectives. First, it teaches athletes to move their limbs quickly. Second, it helps to prevent injuries. Poor technique leads to things like hamstring injuries, shin splints, and, ultimately, slow times. Athletes should spend time working on the technique drills in Chapter 10. Once they get good at them, these drills can be used as warm-up exercises.

Quick Tip for Athletes

> When putting your program together with your coach,
> remember that you get what you train for.

Principle #2: Coaches Have to Make Things More Difficult.

Failing to make workouts more challenging is a classic trap that people fall into when they are training themselves. Most people do a great job of following Principle #1 once it is explained, but Principle #2 is tough for a lot of people. Simply put, people adapt to exercise. If an athlete lifts weights, his muscles adapt by getting larger and stronger.

However, once the body adapts to a given amount of exercise, the individual has to find a way to make that exercise more difficult. Otherwise, his body will stop adapting, which means that he will no longer make gains from his training if he doesn't make it more difficult. Principle #2 is further complicated by the fact that athletes still have to adhere to Principle #1 while making their workouts more difficult.

Training can be made more difficult in several ways:

- Increase the volume
- Increase the intensity
- Change the rest/recovery
- Change the exercises

Increase the Volume

Volume refers to how much work an exerciser does. Increasing the volume can be accomplished by having the athlete perform more repetitions. For example, if an athlete runs five 40-yard sprints on Monday but does six sprints during Tuesday's workout, he will have made the workout more difficult. You can also increase the distance that the athlete runs. For example, he could run 50-yard sprints.

You have to be careful when increasing the volume, because more is not necessarily better. Increasing the distance too greatly (e.g., from 40 yards to 4000 yards) will train the wrong qualities and be counterproductive. Running too many sprints will also be counterproductive because athletes will be too tired to get any quality work done, and this will lead to them running slowly and with bad technique—both of which you want to avoid at all costs.

Increase the Intensity

This guideline is a little deceptive. Every sprint performed to train for the 40 needs to be done with 100 percent intensity. Anything less is training the athlete to run slowly. These sprints can be made more difficult in one of three ways: add resistance, set things up so that the athlete can run faster than he is normally capable of, or vary the speed during the sprint. These three techniques are covered in Chapter 10.

Change the Rest/Recovery

Rest between attempts is going to affect the difficulty of the workout. Running 40-yard sprints with 30 seconds between each sprint is very different from resting for three minutes between each sprint. Changing the duration of the recovery period is another way to make workouts more difficult. However, you have to make sure that athletes are training the correct energy system. Shorten the rest intervals too much and the athletes are training either the glycolytic or the aerobic energy system, which will not benefit their performance in the 40.

Change the Exercises

You can only increase the volume so much before you are in danger of training the wrong qualities. You can only change the intensity so much before athletes run the risk of getting hurt or having an ineffective workout. And you can only change the rest period so much before you begin training the wrong energy system. That said, you can always change the exercises that the athletes perform.

For example, athletes can do sprints from a standing start or from a crouching start. They can also do them from a push-up position. Each variation trains the body a little bit differently. Changing the exercises allows athletes to train the same qualities, but in subtly different ways each time.

How often should you change the exercises? It depends upon the level at which you coach. Beginners through high school athletes need to learn everything from scratch, so they are okay performing the same exercises for up to 12 weeks. Collegiate athletes can perform the same exercises for six to eight weeks. Advanced athletes should change exercises every three to four weeks.

Quick Tip for Athletes

You have to make the workouts harder or you will be wasting your time.

Principle #3: Athletes Must Walk Before They Run.

The process of improving on the 40 is more than just a four-week program. It's a series of steps, each of which builds upon the one that came before. Later chapters cover each type of exercise that athletes can use to improve their performance of the 40. The programs all involve progressions, which basically state that an athlete must master "A" before moving on to "B." This progression is done for two reasons. First, if "A" isn't mastered before attempting "B," then "B" is going to be ineffective because the athlete will not understand how to do it properly. Second, the progression gives the athlete a chance to build a fitness base—in terms of strength, speed, dynamic flexibility, etc.— before moving on to more advanced skills. Without a fitness base, many advanced skills are ineffective or dangerous, which is why an elite athlete's program is not helpful for beginners.

Figure 7-1 presents some general guidelines regarding proper progressions. Keep in mind that these concepts will be detailed in later chapters.

	Varsity Athletes	All-American Athletes	World-Class Athletes
Technique	Ankling drills Butt-kick walks High-knee walks A walks	Varsity athlete drills plus: Butt-kick jogs High-knee skips A skips B walks	All-American drills plus: B skips
Strength	2–3 times per week 60–75% of max	2–3 times per week 70–85% of max	2–3 times per week 70–95% of max
Plyometrics	1–2 times per week Skips Hops	1–2 times per week Skips Hops Bounds	1–2 times per week Skips Hops Bounds One-legged jumps
Acceleration	Falling starts Standing starts Sport-specific starts	Varsity athlete exercises plus: Resisted starts Quickness drills	All-American Athlete exercises
Maximum Velocity	Sprints of 10–200 yards	Sprints of 10–200 yards Varied pace sprints	All-American Athlete exercises plus: Resisted sprinting Assisted sprinting

Figure 7-1. Progressions and appropriate exercise selection based on training experience

Quick Tip for Athletes

Don't be in a rush to get to the advanced workouts.
Get fit and learn so that you don't get hurt.

Principle #4: It Is Hard to Make Gains, but it Is Easy to Lose Them.

Athletes have to work unbelievably hard to improve their 40. However, the moment they stop training, those gains evaporate—and very quickly. They lose muscle mass, strength, speed, and power very quickly after they stop training. In fact, it only takes a matter of weeks for the gains made through training to disappear. For this reason, many athletes perform what is called "active recovery" for two to three weeks after the season ends. Active recovery means that the athlete is performing fun, unstructured workouts that lack the intensity or focus of his normal routine, but keep him in shape nevertheless. In other words, athletes should not just take two or three weeks off after the season ends. Examples of active-recovery work include playing basketball, playing volleyball, running in the pool, and climbing.

> **Quick Tip for Athletes**
>
> Don't waste all that hard work by taking too much time off. You'll quickly lose the gains you've worked so hard to attain.

Principle #5: Properly Putting Everything Together Is Essential.

Subsequent chapters detail the various types of exercises that can improve an athlete's time on the 40, including how to perform them and how to put them together. The basic principles to help coaches learn how to put programs together are as follows. Athletes must:

- Warm up thoroughly
- Work on technique
- Prioritize—speed comes first
- Focus speed workouts on only one quality
- Perform explosive or complicated exercises first
- Get enough rest and recovery

Warm Up Thoroughly

Warming up is very important for preventing injuries and even helps to improve performance. The warm-up should never be skipped or shortened. It should last for 15 to 30 minutes and be performed prior to every workout. The more intense the workout, the more thorough the warm-up needs to be. If the workout is in an extreme environment (e.g., cold, heat), then the warm-up needs to be more thorough to get the body adjusted.

Work on Technique

Technique limits performance in every aspect of sport. Athletes must pay close attention to how to perform each of the exercises in this book and strive for perfection. Not only will it prevent injuries, but it will also help with performance.

Prioritize—Speed Comes First

Speed needs to be the top priority. Everything else takes a back seat to speed training, which means that speed training needs to come first in every workout, before the weights and before the plyometrics. Speed training should be done while athletes are fresh and focused.

Focus Speed Workouts on Only One Quality

Athletes can train the ability to accelerate, the ability to run at maximum speed, or the ability to maintain top speed. Each aspect is trained differently, each requires different things from the athlete's body, and each involves subtly different techniques. Athletes should only train one of those qualities during each workout. Combining these aspects in a single workout tends to confuse the body and interfere with the athlete's gains.

Perform Explosive or Complicated Exercises First

During weight training, the most explosive and complicated exercises need to be done at the beginning of the workout. Performing these exercises at the end of the workout, when the athletes are tired, means that they will be doing them slowly and with bad technique. To be explosive and to have good technique, exercises such as plyometrics and the power clean need to be done at the beginning of a workout while the athletes are fresh.

Get Enough Rest and Recovery

During speed and power training, overtraining is a real risk. Athletes should take one to two days off between speed training, weight training, and plyometric training sessions. Training too frequently will mean that they never fully recover, which is a problem because athletes need that recovery time to adapt to the training.

Make sure your athletes get enough rest in between attempts. They should recover fully between sprints, jumps, and sets in the weight room. Failure to get enough rest will make them so tired that their form will break down and they will slow down—bad things to teach someone who is trying to increase his speed! A general rule of thumb is to have athletes rest for two to three minutes between sets in the weight room and between sprints on the field.

Quick Tip for Athletes

Put your programs together with your coach so that you can be successful.

8

Nutrition, Body Composition, and Rest

Nutrition is probably the most overlooked, yet most influential, aspect of a complete training program. Most athletes don't know what and when to eat. It is not uncommon for athletes to be dehydrated and inadequately fed, and then fizzle out half-way through practice. If athletes want to truly maximize their performance on a 40-yard sprint, they will need to eat right and minimize their body fat. Good sprinters are lean and heavily muscled. Running with excess body fat will inevitably slow an athlete down.

Energy Balance

The second law of thermodynamics, stated in nutritional terms, says that if a person eats more than he expends, he will gain weight. If he eats the same amount as he expends, he will maintain his current weight. If he eats less than he expends, he will lose weight. Times will arise when any athlete may miss a meal or overeat. The body can make an adjustment when necessary, but over time the second law of thermodynamics holds true.

If an athlete is overweight, or more appropriately "overfat," he needs to eat less to shed the excess fat. If he is thin and wants to add additional muscle, he will need to eat more and focus on a strength- and power-training routine. Most athletes at the high school or collegiate level want to change their body composition in some way or another. Before athletes can fully understand the eating strategies, they will need to know a little bit about nutrition.

Essential Nutrients

The human body needs six essential nutrients to function properly: carbohydrates, proteins, fats, vitamins, minerals, and water. Over time, if any one of these essential nutrients is not present, the body will not function to its full capability. Carbohydrates, proteins, and fats are known as the macronutrients. They each provide calories for energy, but they do so in different ways. When training for the 40-yard dash, which requires repeated high-intensity bouts of exercise and all-out effort, it is critical that an athlete chooses the correct proportions of macronutrients.

Carbohydrates

Carbohydrates supply the body with the most efficient source of energy. Their most important function is to supply energy for high-intensity exercise, including sprinting. Carbohydrates are stored in skeletal muscle and the liver, but an endless supply is not available. If exercise is intense and sustained, athletes run out of carbohydrates and performance suffers. This process is called "bonking," and if exercise is continued without eating, athletes will "hit the wall." Athletes who are training for football will commonly fail to replace carbohydrate stores after training. Over several days of two-a-day workouts, carbohydrates are continually depleted and never replaced to optimal levels. This condition can lead to fatigue, dehydration, heat illness, and injury. Good choices for carbohydrates include cereal, bread, pasta, fruits, and vegetables.

> **Quick Tip for Athletes**
>
> Carbohydrates should make up about 55 to 65 percent of the total calories in your diet.

Protein

Protein is used to build and repair body tissue, most notably muscle. When training for speed, strength, and power, additional muscle equates to athletes being bigger, stronger, and faster. A word of caution: Additional or excess protein in the diet will not translate to additional muscle. Eating lots of extra protein won't create extra muscle mass. Instead, it will become extra fat or be lost when the athletes goes to the bathroom.

Protein is made up of amino acids. The body needs 22 different amino acids to perform properly. The amino acids that the body can manufacture itself are called nonessential amino acids. The essential amino acids must be consumed in the diet. Teach your athletes that buying amino-acid supplements over the counter in an attempt to improve strength and power is futile. The body needs to combine all of the amino acids in the correct ratios to build and rebuild muscle. Excess amino acids will ultimately be flushed from the body in the urine.

It is important to eat high-quality protein that contains amino acids that the body can easily assimilate. Animal and dairy proteins are typically the best choices, including fish, chicken, lean cuts of red meat, and non- or low-fat dairy products. As a quick measure to determine if an athlete is getting enough protein in his diet, remember that his body weight in pounds should be about the same as the total number of grams of protein consumed each day.

Quick Tip for Athletes

Dietary protein should make up about 20 to 25 percent of your total calories.

Fats

Fats are necessary for the body because they insulate the vital organs and are an endless supply of energy should an individual need it. Sprinting short distances does not require the use of fats for energy. Generally speaking, if a person eats lots of fats in his diet, he will be fat. Fat below the skin—called subcutaneous fat—is counterproductive to moving quickly, not only for sprinting but also on the field. If an athlete wants to run fast, he will need to keep his body fat to a minimum. Fat in the diet comes in several forms, including salad dressings, fried foods, whole-milk products, butter, oils, and most desserts.

Quick Tip for Athletes

Keep dietary fat intake under 25 percent of total calories and you will be leaner, meaner, and faster.

Macronutrient	Basic Function	Sources
Carbohydrates	Supply the body with energy for intense exercise; used by the central nervous system	Whole grains, vegetables, fruits, breads, and pastas
Proteins	Build and rebuild muscle tissue	Lean cuts of red meat, poultry, fish, and low- to nonfat milk products
Fats	Protect vital organs and serve as an abundant source of energy	Whole-milk products, ice cream, cheeses, and salad dressings

Figure 8-1. Macronutrients summary

Quick Tip for Athletes

Nutrition plays a critical role in your training program. Get in touch with a sports nutritionist or read up on the topic for more information.

In addition to the three macronutrients, the body needs micronutrients to function properly. These nutrients are important, but they are needed in much smaller amounts than carbohydrates, proteins, and fats. Micronutrients include both vitamins and minerals.

Vitamins

The body uses two kinds of vitamins: water-soluble and fat-soluble. The water-soluble vitamins, including the B-complex vitamins and vitamin C, are used to assist in the production of energy. The fat-soluble vitamins serve important functions, but can be toxic in the body if taken in abundance over time. A well-balanced diet rich in fruits, vegetables, and lean red meat will ensure that all of the necessary vitamins are available for the body to use.

Minerals

The body needs 22 naturally occurring minerals, which are found in oceans, streams, and lakes. Plants take up minerals, so when people eat the plants (or the animals that eat the plants) they get minerals in the diet. These minerals assist the body in many of its functions, such as the formation of bones and teeth, proper functioning of the nervous system, and enzyme activity during energy production.

Water

Approximately 70 percent of the human body is made up of water, and virtually all bodily functions take place in a water medium. Many individuals overlook water consumption because they think that they get enough in the form of other liquids, such as fruit juices, sport drinks, milk, soft drinks, and in fruits and vegetables. During heavy training, the body can fairly easily lose 2 to 3 percent of total body weight. Drinking water before, during, and after training will ensure an efficiently functioning metabolism and aid in body cooling and recovery. If bodyweight is being lost during training, it is best to get it back to normal levels before subsequent training. If body weight does not return to pretraining levels, the athlete is in a state of dehydration, which can lead to various forms of heat illness.

Other Dietary Concerns

How food is prepared can have a tremendous impact on calories and where those calories are coming from. Most people think fried food tastes great, but the fat content goes up exponentially when food is fried. Generally speaking, athletes should choose grilled and baked foods and remove the skin from poultry.

Breakfast

If an athlete trains for long periods of time and at a high intensity, his body is undoubtedly going to need energy to sustain that effort. An athlete must eat breakfast for several reasons, especially if he is training in the morning:

- To cap off energy stores before training
- To have protein and carbohydrates available to speed recovery
- To elevate low blood glucose levels, which will make him feel better and more prepared to train

In addition, an athlete must be sure to drink plenty of water with breakfast, because the body needs to be rehydrated after a night of sleep. This additional water will ensure proper functioning of the body's metabolism and potentially delay dehydration.

Meal Timing

The timing of meals can have huge implications on training and recovery time. "Windows" of metabolic opportunity exist that can maximize training and nutritional impact. These times occur before, during, and after training and practice.

- Before: An athlete must be sure to fill up his fuel tank with a moderately sized meal two to four hours before training. He should eat a fairly high-carbohydrate, moderate-protein, and low-fat meal at this time. Within 30 to 60 minutes of the training session, the athlete should "top off" the fuel tank with a light carbohydrate/protein snack. He must always drink water during this period as well.
- During: Athletes must keep consuming fluids during training and practice. Water is a must, though sports drinks and energy gels are good choices as well.
- After: Athletes must eat immediately after training. If they wait longer than 30 to 45 minutes after the end of the training session, the best opportunity to take advantage of the body's physiological response is lost. A 200-calorie meal with a ratio of three grams of carbohydrate to one gram of protein is optimal. In addition, 20 ounces of skim milk is perfect at this time. Within another one-and-a-half to two-and-a-half hours, athletes should eat a low-fat, balanced meal to ensure recovery to a greater extent. Again, athletes must continue to consume water.

Quick Tip for Athletes

Pay particular attention to the meals before, during, and immediately after training.

Low-Carbohydrate Diets

No discussion on nutrition is complete without covering the low-carbohydrate diet craze. "Low-carb" diets are popular with the general public for various reasons, including the multimillion dollar marketing campaigns, the quick loss in body weight, and the fact that tasty foods can be included in the diet. Because high-intensity training for strength and power requires carbohydrates, a low-carb diet is a recipe for disaster for any athlete.

Quick Tip for Athletes

> If you are interested in sport performance, a low-carb diet is a colossal waste of time and energy and is counterproductive to hard training.

Supplements

The three primary considerations when selecting a supplement are as follows:

- Is it safe?
- Is it legal?
- Does it work?

In a study conducted by the International Olympic Committee, the contents of more than 600 sport supplements were analyzed. Of the supplements investigated in the United States, more than 28 percent were contaminated with a substance that was not listed on the label. These contaminates could lead to the athlete testing positive for a banned substance. Very few sport supplements actually work, and of those that do only a certain percentage of the population will respond favorably. The bottom line is that athletes must proceed with caution when considering supplementation.

Quick Tip for Athletes

> Rely on food, not supplements, to get the nutrients you need.
> Be extremely cautious with supplements.

Rest

Rest consists of the time between training sessions. The amount of rest needed depends on several factors, including the following:

- Fitness level: The higher an athlete's fitness level, the less rest he needs between training sessions.

- Fatigue level: The more tired an athlete gets from individual workouts, the more rest he will need before engaging in another workout.
- Individual capability to recover: Everyone is different in this regard. Some people can bounce back very quickly from an intense training session, while others cannot, which is one more reason why programs must be individualized.
- Nutritional status: If an athlete doesn't provide his body with the fuel it needs, he will not be able to recover from the workouts as quickly.
- Previous training volume and intensity: Training is cumulative, which means that what an athlete did yesterday affects what he can do today. If he is coming off a high-volume or high-intensity phase, he will probably need more rest.
- Environmental conditions, such as heat and humidity: Excessive heat and humidity will sap an athlete's ability to train until he becomes acclimated.
- Outside stress, such as personal life, sleep, and school: Unfortunately, the real world often interferes with training and can have a positive or a negative effect on an athlete's ability to train and recover.

As a general rule, a beginner will need more rest than someone at a higher level of fitness. Three training sessions per week is probably ideal for beginners. As athletes become more fit, they can incur higher volumes and intensities of training and workout frequency can move up to four to five days per week. World-class and professional athletes often train two or three times per day, six or seven days per week, for a total of more that 14 physical-conditioning sessions per week.

If an athlete is just starting an off-season training program, it is much wiser to gradually begin the training over a few weeks, as opposed to trying too much, too early. Starting at a level beyond an athlete's physical capabilities can lead to injury, fatigue, overtraining, and ultimately poor performance.

Quick Tip for Athletes

It is easier to adjust a training schedule for more intensity and higher-volume workouts, as opposed to overestimating your capabilities at first and then having to cut back.

9

Warming Up

Lack of time can never be an excuse to skip the warm-up. If an athlete doesn't have time to properly warm up, then he doesn't have time to work out. The warm-up is critical to preventing injuries during training and to performing at maximum capacity. Athletes must take the time to warm up properly and use this time to focus mentally on the subsequent workout. The warm-up time can also be used to work on technique. The warm-up has two basic phases: the general warm-up and the specific warm-up.

The General Warm-Up

The general warm-up has several purposes, including the following:

- Warming the muscular system: This warming is accomplished by pumping blood into the muscles, creating friction from the contraction of myofilaments, and generating heat from the energy process.
- Lubricating joints: This task is accomplished by increasing blood flow through the joints.
- Oxygenating blood and active muscle: As an athlete warms up, his heart rate increases, thereby pumping more blood into the muscles. The body also opens up "extra" capillaries to get more blood into the muscles.
- Mentally preparing for the training session: By starting slowly and gradually increasing the intensity and speed of the exercises, the athlete gets a chance to mentally prepare for the training session.
- Stimulating the nervous system: It is difficult to go from complete rest to explosive action. Gradually increasing the complexity and speed of the exercises allows the athlete's nervous system to be more explosive during the training session.

The general warm-up consists of whole-body movements such as jogging and some dynamic flexibility drills. It starts out at a low intensity and gradually increases in intensity, though it never gets to a high intensity. The goal is to get a light sweat going during the general warm-up.

The Specific Warm-Up

When training for the 40, the specific warm-up should specifically target sprinting, which means that it should train the muscles in ways similar to how they will be used during sprinting. It should also train the components of the sprinting movement and pick up in terms of speed and intensity as it progresses.

Quick Tip for Athletes

> The amount of time spent warming up will vary depending on fitness level. Typically, the more fit the individual, the longer it will take to warm up.

Dynamic Flexibility

Dynamic flexibility exercises are important because performing static stretches prior to a speed workout is counterproductive and could be dangerous. Dynamic flexibility exercises train for flexibility while the body is moving. These stretches are held only for a second or two, which differs from static stretches that are typically held for 30 seconds or more. Dynamic flexibility routines have been proven to not only be more effective than static stretching routines, but also to decrease the chances of injury. The dynamic stretching routine presented in this section can be completed before form-running drills or incorporated into them.

Walking Lunge (Figure 9-1)

In this exercise, the athlete places his hands on his hips and performs a deep knee bend toward the ground with each step. He should lunge for about 10 to 15 yards. As a variation, he can lunge backward as well.

Walking Lunge With Torso Rotation (Figure 9-2)

The athlete places his hands behind his head and rotates the torso forward and down, touching the elbow to the opposite knee with each step. He should lunge for 10 to 15 yards. As a variation, he can lunge and rotate backward as well.

Figure 9-1

Figure 9-2

Side Lunges (Figure 9-3)

The athlete simply takes a large step to one side and squats down until he feels a stretch in his groin. He should lunge for about 10 yards and be sure to lunge to both sides.

Figure 9-3

Spider Crawls (Figure 9-4)

Have the athlete get down on all fours and exaggerate a crawling motion. He should crawl for about 10 yards. As a variation, he can crawl to the sides and back as well.

Figure 9-4

Hip Flexor/Hamstring Stretch (Figure 9-5)

To stretch the hip flexors (at the front of the hip), the athlete places one foot in front, with the torso upright. He leans forward, keeping his abdominal muscles tight. He holds the position for two or three seconds. Before switching sides, he can sit back and stretch the opposite hamstring. Instead of holding the stretch position for 30 seconds or so, he should hold it for only two or three seconds and cycle back and forth on each leg.

Figure 9-5

Arm Circles Forward and Backward (Figure 9-6)

The athlete completes this stretch from the standing position. He simply circles his arms in both directions, making circles in a controlled manner and being sure not to swing the arms too quickly.

Figure 9-6

Knees to Chest (Figure 9-7)

The athlete lifts one knee up to his chest and pulls it slightly in. He holds the position for two or three seconds before alternating to the other side. He walks forward for 10 to 15 yards. As a variation, incorporate a lunge between each time he pulls the knee up.

Figure 9-6

Walking Glute Stretch (Figure 9-8)

This movement is a variation of the knees to chest stretch. Instead of pulling the knee to the chest, the athlete grabs his lower leg and pulls directly upward. He will feel the stretch in the glutes and the outside of the upper thigh.

Figure 9-6

10

Running Fast to Be Fast

It may sound obvious, but athletes have to practice running fast to get better at it. Sometimes people get so obsessed with all of the other tools that they overlook the obvious. Running fast is a skill, and it must be practiced. This chapter presents some tools to teach athletes how to learn to run fast, describes exercises to train those first few steps, describes how to train for top speed, and presents some recommendations on how to put all of this information together.

Learning How to Run Fast

An ideal technique exists for sprinting—as covered in Chapters 4, 5, and 6. Exercises can be used to help reinforce good running technique. Think of these exercises as a series of steps, or progressions. Each step builds onto the one that came before it. Once these exercises are mastered, they can be used as part of the warm-up. The steps for learning how to sprint fast are as follows:

- Learn what to do with the arms
- Learn how to lift the foot off the ground
- Learn how to bring the heel to the hip
- Learn how to step over the opposite knee
- Learn how to strike the ground

Using the Arms (Figure 10-1)

To learn this motion, the athlete must sit down on the ground and extend his legs out in front. He sits up nice and tall (chest out, shoulders back). He should start off with one hand next to his hip and one in front of his shoulder. He performs this drill by pumping his arms forward and backward, as if he was running. This drill can be performed for 10 to 20 seconds. Normally, this drill is only used during the first training session, but if arm swing is a problem, then use it as needed.

Figure 10-1

Coaching Cues

- Keep the arms tight to the body.
- Drive the arms back.
- Move the hand from the hips to the shoulders.
- Swing the arm from the shoulders, not the elbows.

Lifting the Foot off the Ground (Figure 10-2)

This drill, which is called ankling, is performed while walking over 10 to 20 yards. The athlete takes a step forward with his left leg. As the hips move forward, he allows the right foot to point until it breaks contact with the ground. As the foot leaves the ground, he casts his right foot. Keeping the foot cast, he swings the right foot forward from the hips (keeping the knees stiff). The right foot should hit the ground just in front of the hips, with the ball of the foot landing on the ground. The athlete must perform this drill with the left side as well. He should repeat the movement over 10 to 20 yards. Note that advanced athletes can perform this drill as a fast skip, in which case the exercise is called a straight-leg bound.

Figure 10-2

Coaching Cues

- Stay tall.
- Allow the right foot to point before it breaks contact with the ground.
- Cast the right foot after it leaves the ground.
- Swing the right leg forward from the hips.
- The ball of the right foot contacts the ground.

Bringing the Heel to the Hip (Figure 10-3)

This drill is sometimes called a heel kick and is performed over 10 to 20 yards. The athlete begins by stepping forward with the left foot. As the hips move forward, he casts his right ankle. Immediately after casting the right ankle, he brings the right heel up to the right hip by trying to slide the heel up an imaginary wall behind him. In other words, if he does this drill properly, the knee will travel forward and he'll have about a 45-degree angle at the right hip. He then places his right foot on the ground, with the ball of that foot striking the ground. Be sure to have him repeat the drill with the left side as well. Advanced athletes can also perform this drill as a run.

Figure 10-3

Coaching Cues

- Stay tall.
- Cast the right foot as it leaves the ground.
- Slide the right heel up to the right hip.
- Form a 45-degree angle at the right hip.
- Keep the foot cast.

Stepping Over the Opposite Knee (Figure 10-4)

This drill is called a high knee drill and is performed over 10 to 20 yards. The athlete lifts his right foot off the ground so that it is higher than the left knee. As he lifts the right knee, make sure that his right foot is cast. He then steps forward and places the right foot on the ground (still cast) so that the ball of the foot strikes the ground. Be sure to have him repeat this drill to the left side. Advanced athletes should do this as a skip.

Figure 10-4

Coaching Cues

- Stay tall.
- Keep the foot cast.
- Lift the right foot higher than the left knee.
- Drive the right foot toward the ground, using the glutes.
- The ball of the right foot should strike the ground.

Striking the Ground (Figure 10-5)

This drill is called an "A" drill and is performed over 10 to 20 yards. This exercise combines heel kicks with the high knee drill. Have the athlete perform a heel kick with his right leg (i.e., bring the heel to the hip), then raise his right foot so that it is higher than the left knee. He then drives the right foot to the ground, just in front of the hips, using the glutes. The ball of the foot should strike the ground. Be sure to have him repeat this drill to the left side.

Figure 10-5

Coaching Cues

- Stay tall.
- Keep the foot cast.
- Slide the right heel up to the right hip.
- Step over the left knee with the right foot.
- Drive the right foot down using the glutes.
- The ball of the right foot should strike the ground.

The First Few Steps

The technique drills are great for developing fundamental techniques. However, they are not a substitute for actual sprinting. This section explains how to train the first few steps of the sprint, which are critical to a good 40 time.

You want to train two distinct components when it comes to taking the first few steps. First, athletes must take the first step as explosively as possible. Doing so gives him a head start and a better chance to get to the finish line faster. Second, since athletes don't have much time during the 40, they must work to quickly increase speed.

Explosively Taking the First Step

Most people don't know how to be explosive with their first step. Before beginning drills that address this aspect of the sprint, athletes must figure out which foot should be back. Have them stand up and cross both arms across the chest (Figure 10-6). Which arm is directly against the chest? That arm corresponds to the leg that athletes want to put behind them when getting into position to do the first drill.

Figure 10-6

For the first drill, called falling starts, the athlete stands up tall and faces the course. He lines his toes up on the start line. Keeping the feet close together (no more than hip-width apart), he slides the back foot back so that the toes are even with the heel of the front foot (Figure 10-7). From this position, he bends his knees slightly. Keeping the trunk straight, he bends forward from the hips and allows his arms to hang down (Figure 10-8).

From this position, he relaxes and leans forward. As he does so, he will begin to fall forward, which is okay. He should allow the falling motion to happen. As he falls forward, he will naturally step forward with the back foot. This step is the first explosive step. As that back foot steps forward, he should drive the knee up and drive that arm backward hard. The athlete then prints the desired distance from the falling start.

Figure 10-7

Figure 10-8

Once the athlete is very comfortable with falling starts, it's time to advance to the next drill—standing starts. He should assume the same starting position, but instead of letting himself fall forward, he drives that back knee forward and drives the arm back hard. Again, he must sprint the desired distance.

Accelerating

Learning how to accelerate is extremely important, especially since the majority of the 40 is spent accelerating. Athletes can learn this skill by performing sprints over short distances (generally five to 20 yards). As an athlete is performing these short sprints, he should focus on the start. He should take that first step as explosively as possible. He can also vary the starting position, but the motion of the back knee and the arm drive must remain consistent. Have him start from a three- or four-point stance, from the push-up position, and with his back to the course (i.e., turn around and then sprint).

As he is running these short-distance sprints, he should focus on several things. First, he should keep his foot cast. Second, he must land on the ball of his foot. Third, he must pick his knees up. Finally, he must use his arms properly.

Taking the first step explosively and then running the first half of the 40 will definitely get an athlete started. However, a certain part of the 40 is concerned with top speed. The next part of this chapter explains about how to train for top speed.

Quick Tip for Athletes

Starting properly entails four fundamental aspects:

- Take the first step explosively
- Keep the foot cast
- Pick up the knees
- Use the arms

Top Speed

Top speed is as fast as an athlete can run. He may never get there during the 40 (it takes an elite sprinter six or seven seconds to reach top speed). However, as soon as he gets past 10 to 20 yards, he should begin running as though he is at top speed. See Chapter 6 for a discussion of proper technique when running at top speed. Athletes can use four tools to train for top speed:

- Just run

- Vary the speed
- Run faster than you can
- Make things more difficult

Just Run

If an athlete wants to get better at running at top speed, he has to practice that aspect of the sprint, which requires running sprints of between 20 and 100 yards while focusing on speed and technique. Every sprint should be run at close to 100 percent. If an athlete runs sprints with less than 100 percent effort, then he is learning to run sprints slowly.

The bulk of sprint training should be spent performing these types of sprints. The tools that follow are for intermediate and advanced athletes.

Vary the Speed

Changing the speed during the sprint teaches the athlete how to run relaxed while at top speed (so that his limbs can continue moving quickly without too much resistance). It also teaches him how to change gears in the middle of a sprint.

The easiest way to vary the speed is with a flying sprint. Mark out a course, assuming that the first 20 to 30 yards will be an acceleration zone and the last 10 yards or so will be a top speed zone. While the athlete is running in the acceleration zone, he must work on increasing his speed. The moment he hits the top speed zone, he should be running as fast as he can.

These sprints can also be strung together as drills called "ins and outs." The athletes work through a course with a 20- to 30-yard acceleration zone, followed by a 10-yard acceleration zone, followed by another 20- to 30-yard acceleration zone, followed by another 10-yard acceleration zone, etc. These drills are very tiring, to say the least.

Run Faster Than You Can

Believe it or not, it is actually possible for an athlete to run faster than he is normally capable of. This type of drill is sometimes called assisted sprinting. Have something (or someone) that is faster than the exercising athlete pull him. You could use a faster athlete, a car, or a bungee cord attached to something that won't move. This drill lets the athlete practice moving his limbs faster than he normally can, which will hopefully transfer over to running without assistance.

Be very careful with this training tool. You do not want athletes running much faster than 105 percent of their normal speed, because their form will break down and it could result in bad habits.

Make Things More Difficult

Just as techniques can be used to make sprinting easier, sprinting can be made more difficult by adding some sort of drag that weighs the runner down. This resistance could be in the form of a parachute, a tire, a weighted sled, running uphill, etc. Running with resistance teaches the athlete to recruit more muscles to perform the sprint, which will hopefully carry over to his normal sprints. It's usually best to only do these sprints for 10 to 20 yards. Watch the athlete's form very carefully. If you see someone leaning forward, then you have too much resistance. Resistance should not slow the athlete down by more than 10 percent. Additional resistance may lead to bad habits.

Quick Tip for Athletes

> You have to practice running fast! Drills and other exercises have a role, but you have to actually practice running sprints fast to get good at them.

Putting Everything Together

Workouts should focus on acceleration or top speed—never both. Each skill requires different responses from the nervous system and you are trying to optimize each athlete's training time.

It is usually best for workouts to focus on one exercise or distance. For example, if an athlete is performing 60-yard sprints to work on top speed, then that should be the focus of the workout. It would not be appropriate to do five 60-yard sprints, then five 100-yard sprints. Advanced athletes can break this rule, but beginners never should.

When an athlete's speed or form begins to suffer, stop the session immediately. Teaching an athlete to run slowly or with bad technique is not smart. Sprinting sessions should be short, intense, and effective. They should not be gut checks and athletes should not be absolutely exhausted at the end of a training session.

Now that you understand some of the tools used in speed training, the rest of this book covers different tools that will help supplement this speed training. Finally, the final chapter will present some sample workout programs for different levels of athletes.

11

Strength Training

Strength is extremely important for running a fast 40. Strength enables an athlete to maintain good posture, be explosive, and exert force against the ground. Lifting weights is the best means of developing the needed strength. While many other exercises could be performed, athletes should focus on the following fundamental exercises as the foundation of a lifting program designed to improve the strength needed to run a fast 40.

- Power clean
- Bench press
- Back squat
- Pull-ups
- Overhead press
- Romanian dead lift

Each of these exercises incorporates large muscle groups:

- The power clean uses almost every muscle in the body.
- The bench press uses the muscles of the chest, shoulders, and triceps.
- Back squats develop almost every muscle from the waist down.
- Pull-ups develop the muscles of the upper back, shoulders, and biceps.
- The overhead press works the muscles of the shoulders and triceps and also requires that the lower back become stronger.
- The Romanian dead lift develops the hamstrings, glutes, and lower back.

In addition, these exercises can be performed using free weights, which means that they incorporate more complex motor abilities. Many motions have to be integrated, executed, and balanced to perform each of these exercises. Not only will they develop muscles strength, but these exercises will also help to develop balance, mobility, and coordination.

These exercises also elicit a great hormonal response, creating an anabolic, or strength-building, environment. Aside from the bench press and pull-up, these exercises are ground-based movements, which means that they may have greater transfer to activities that involve exerting force against the ground, including sprinting. Note that wearing a pair of weight lifting shoes to perform the ground-based lifts will give athletes better support and stability (Figure 11-1). Finally, these exercises elicit high force and power outputs that closely simulate sport-specific movements.

Figure 11-1. Weight lifting shoes provide support and stability.

A more explosive and strong muscle will undoubtedly generate more force than a slower, weaker one. Biomechanical analysis of running reveals that the ability to overcome vertical forces is much more important than the ability to overcome horizontal forces. This fact is one of the primary reasons for using explosive vertical weight-training exercises like the Olympic lifts.

Quick Tip for Athletes

Weight training should complement training for your sport,
not compete with it or be the focus of training.

Quick Tip for Athletes

When training for high performance, athletes and coaches should
look for maximal results, not just positive results.

Exercise Descriptions

For safety and effectiveness, it is very important that each of the following exercises is performed correctly. Performing the exercises incorrectly, or using bad form to lift a few extra pounds, will often lead to injury.

Power Clean*

Start Position (Figure 11-2)

- The balls of the feet are directly below the bar.
- The feet are shoulder width-apart.
- The hands are slightly wider than shoulder-width apart.
- The back is flat and the head is tilted slightly up.
- The hips are below the shoulders, with the back at approximately a 45-degree angle.
- The elbows are pointed outward.

First Pull (Figure 11-3)

- The athlete extends at the knees and hips to raise the bar to knee level. Make sure the hips and shoulders rise at the same speed.

Second Pull (Figures 11-4 and 11-5)

- As the bar passes the knees, the chest should remain slightly in front of the bar.
- Once the bar has reached the lower thighs, the athlete raises the chest.
- He must keep the bar in contact with the thighs.

---

* Caution: If you do not know how to teach this lift, find a coach who can show you proper technique.

- Once the bar is at mid-thigh level, he violently extends the body upward.
- The athlete finishes the second pull by shrugging and extending on the toes.

Figure 11-2

Figure 11-3

Figure 11-4

Figure 11-5

The Catch (Figure 11-6)

- The athlete must let the elbows point outward while dipping into a one-quarter squat position.
- He then quickly moves the elbows around the bar and receives the weight on the front of the shoulders.

Figure 11-6

The Finish (Figure 11-7)

- The athlete stands with the bar on the front of the shoulder with the elbows high.

Key Points

- The back must be flat and neutral throughout the movement.
- The athlete must finish the second pull by fully extending.
- He must not bend the arms before fully extending.
- Use a platform and bumper plates for this movement.

Figure 11-7

Back Squat*

Start/Finish Position (Figure 11-8)

- The feet are shoulder-width apart.
- The bar is placed on the upper back.
- The hands are outside of the shoulders with a closed grip.
- The head is neutral and the eyes are looking straight ahead.

Midpoint (Figure 11-9)

- The athlete begins the descent by moving the hips backward and then immediately bending at the knees.
- The back must remain flat.
- The midpoint is reached with the crease on the front of the thighs is level with the top of the knees.
- The athlete should return to the starting position in the same path as the descent.

*Caution: Always use a spotter for this lift.

Figure 11-8

Figure 11-9

Key points

- The back must remain flat and in a neutral position.
- The athlete must not let the hips shift backward on the way up.

Bench Press*

Start/Finish Position (Figure 11-10)

- The athlete must lie down on the bench.
- Five points of contact should exist during the bench press: head, shoulders, hips, and both feet. The five points must remain in contact throughout the movement.
- The athlete should use a closed grip to hold the bar.
- The hands are placed slightly wider than shoulder-width apart.
- The bar starts directly above the shoulders.
- The arms are fully extended.

Figure 11-10
*Caution: Always use a spotter for this lift.

Midpoint (Figure 11-11)

- The athlete begins the descent by bending at the elbows and arcing the bar toward the lower part of the chest.
- The midpoint is reached when the bar touches the lower chest below the nipples.
- The athlete must return to the starting position in the same path as the descent.

Figure 11-11

Key Points

- The athlete must not bounce the bar off the chest.
- The five points of contact must remain in place.

Pull-Ups

Start/Finish Position (Figure 11-12)

- The athlete uses an overhand, shoulder-width grip.
- The elbows are fully extended.

Figure 11-12

Midpoint (Figure 11-13)

- The athlete begins the ascent by bending at the elbows, raising his body.
- The head must be held slightly back to avoid hitting the bar.
- The midpoint is reached with the chin is above the bar.

Figure 11-13

Key Point

- The athlete must not swing or use momentum to come out of the bottom position.

Standing Overhead Press

Start/Finish Position (Figure 11-14)

- The feet are shoulder-width apart.
- The bar is placed on the front of the shoulders.
- The hands are outside of the shoulders with a closed grip.
- The head is neutral and the eyes are looking straight ahead.
- The elbows are slightly in front of the bar.

Figure 11-14

Midpoint (Figure 11-15)

- The athlete begins the movement by extending the arms and brining the head back to avoid hitting the bar.
- The athlete must keep the bar positioned over the shoulders.

- The midpoint is reached when the arms are fully extended and the head is back under the bar.

Figure 11-15

Key Points

- The athlete must not initiate the movement by bending and extending at the knees.
- Use a platform and bumper plates for this movement.

Romanian Dead Lifts

Start/Finish Position (Figure 11-16)

- The athlete holds a bar in front of the thighs with the feet shoulder-width apart.
- The shoulders must be back and the chest up.
- He must bend the knees slightly and hold that angle for the duration of the movement.

Midpoint (Figure 11-17)

- The athlete begins the movement by letting his hips "push" back.

- He then slides the bar down the thighs, keeping the back flat and neutral.
- The midpoint is reached when a slight stretch is felt in the hamstrings.

Figure 11-16

Figure 11-17

Key Points

- Do not use much weight for this exercise. Start very conservatively. The athlete will probably feel a little sore the next day.
- The knee angle must be maintained for the duration of the movement.
- A flat and neutral back position must be maintained.

12

Plyometrics

Plyometrics, or "plyos," are basically hopping, skipping, jumping, and leaping exercises. These exercises use a fast "stretch-shortening cycle" to elicit a high-force, high-speed, neuromuscular response. Plyometrics can train an athlete's body in ways that other exercises cannot. Plyometrics are also an excellent complement to speed training.

It is important that the surface upon which plyometrics are performed is forgiving. Flat natural grass works great, as do synthetic athletic fields and running tracks. If you need to train your athletes inside, a wrestling mat also works well. A basketball court is not perfect, but also can work. Never perform plyometrics on concrete or pavement.

The plyometric exercises described in this chapter will enhance and maximize running speed. All athletes should start with the low-level movements and gradually progress to the high-level plyometrics.

Quick Tip for Athletes

"Low-level plyometrics" doesn't mean low intensity. The low-level movements should be mastered first before moving up the more advanced plyometric exercises.

Low-Level Plyometrics

Double-Leg Hops, Single Response (Standing Broad Jump) (Figures 12-1 through 12-3)

Description: A double-leg hop is one of the fundamental movements that all athletes can learn. Many athletes probably already know how to execute this movement.

Start: The feet are shoulder-width apart. The athlete makes a quick countermovement with the arms while bending into a quarter-squat. He then explodes quickly, taking off from the ground at a 45-degree angle. He must be sure to extend fully at the hips and knees.

Finish: The athlete should land softly with the feet shoulder-width apart—in the starting position.

Figure 12-1

Figure 12-2

Figure 12-3

Box Jumps (Figures 12-4 through 12-6)

Description: Box jumps are easy to execute and really emphasize the triple extension of the knees, hips, and ankles.

Start: The athlete stands in front of a box approximately arm's length away. The box should be high enough that he can easily land on top in a near quarter-squat position. The feet are shoulder-width apart. He must explode quickly, taking off from the ground at an angle that will allow him to land on the box. He must be sure to extend fully at the hips and knees.

Finish: The athlete should land softly, with the feet shoulder-width apart on the box, and then step down (not jump down).

Figure 12-4

Figure 12-5

Figure 12-6

90/90 Touches, Single Response (Figures 12-7 and 12-8)

Description: A 90/90 touch is fairly simple to perform and does not require any equipment. It is also easy for the beginner exerciser to learn.

Start: The athlete stands with the feet shoulder-width apart and the elbows bent at 90 degrees, palms facing down. He makes a quick countermovement down by bending at the knees and hips and then jumps straight up. He pulls the feet up to the hips and brings the thighs to the hands, creating a 90-degree angle between the hips and torso.

Finish: The athlete should land softly with the feet shoulder-width apart—in the starting position.

Figure 12-7

Figure 12-8

Power Skips (Figure 12-9)

Description: Power skips involve skipping with as much height and distance as possible. An athlete will need approximately 20 to 30 yards of open space to execute the power skip.

Start: The athlete begins by skipping at a "normal" height. After a couple of contacts on each side, he drives off the ground to add height and distance. He should get as high as possible.

Finish: The power skip is finished after the selected distance is completed.

Figure 12-9

Intermediate-Level Plyometrics

Double-Leg Hops Over Cones (Figures 12-10 through 12-12)

Description: Double-leg hops over cones are simple and effective once the athlete has mastered the low-level plyometrics. Set up four to eight cones in a straight line with approximately one yard between cones. The cones serve as markets for this exercise.

Start: The athlete stands in front of the first cone with a shoulder-width stance. He jumps as high as possible and uses his arms to "block" the upward movement. To "block" the movement, he simply stops his arms at a given point. This "block" transfers the energy of the arms to the jump height.

Landing: The athlete should land in a quarter-squat position between cones and quickly take off for the next repetition.

Finish: The set is complete after the athlete has jumped over all of the cones.

Figure 12-10

Figure 12-11

Figure 12-12

Chest Tucks, Single Response (Figures 12-13 and 12-14)

Description: The chest tuck emphasizes the hips flexing to the torso, and adds some body coordination as well.

Start: The athlete makes a quick countermovement from a standing position with the feet shoulder-width apart. He explodes off the ground and blocks the arms at about shoulder level. He then brings the knees up to the chest in a "tuck" position. He should try to wrap his arms around his shins at the highest point of the jump.

Landing: The athlete should land in a quarter-squat position between repetitions and quickly take off to begin the next jump.

Finish: The set is completed after four to eight repetitions have been performed.

Figure 12-13

Figure 12-14

Step-Up Jump (Figures 12-15 and 12-16)

Description: Use a box height that creates a 90-degree angle at the hips and knees in the start position.

Start: The athlete begins the movement by placing one foot on the box and the other on the ground. He performs a countermovement with the arms and leans forward with the chest. He then explodes off the box, driving upward with the take-off leg.

Landing: The athlete should land with the take-off leg in the same position as at the start, and then quickly execute the next repetition.

Finish: The set is completed after four to eight repetitions have been performed.

Figure 12-15

Figure 12-16

High-Level Plyometrics

Alternate Bounds (Figure 12-17)

Description: Alternate bounds entail bounding from one leg to the other in a running fashion.

Start: The athlete begins by running at a medium speed and exaggerates the running stride and leg lift.

Landing: Ground-contact time should be minimal and explosive.

Finish: The set is completed after the specified distance or after four or five contacts have been made on each leg.

Caution: This movement is not recommended for heavier athletes (e.g., offensive and defensive linemen).

Figure 12-17

Single-Leg Bounds (Figure 12-18)

Description: Single-leg bounds involve bounding on one leg at a time. This exercise is an advanced movement and athletes may need time to develop explosive technique.

Start: The athlete begins by running at a slow pace and then cycles the contact leg instead of alternating.

Landing: Ground-contact time should be minimal and explosive.

Finish: The set is completed after the specified distance or after four or five contacts have been made on the drive leg.

Depth Jump to Box (Figures 12-19 through 12-21)

Description: A depth jump is a form of plyometric exercise called "shock methodology." The shock is to the nervous system. Jumping down from the correct height can produce significant results. The box height should be approximately 12 to 18 inches. If you are not sure, err on the side of caution and use a lower box height. Begin this exercise with two boxes set up three to four feet apart.

Start: The athlete stands on the first box and steps off with the feet shoulder-width apart.

Landing: The athlete should land in a quarter-squat position with the feet shoulder-width apart. He should make a quick countermovement with the arms and explode onto the second box.

Finish: The athlete should be able to land in a quarter-squat position on the second box. He must land softly, with the feet shoulder-width apart on the box and then step down.

Figure 12-18

Figure 12-19

Figure 12-20

Figure 12-20

13

Staying Healthy

A certain number of athletes will get hurt after starting a sprinting program. An injured athlete is obviously not a very effective athlete. This chapter examines three of the most common injuries that people suffer during sprinting programs and explains how to avoid and manage them.

Delayed Onset Muscle Soreness

Any time that an athlete begins an exercise program, it is very likely that he will experience muscle soreness. The immediate muscle soreness and fatigue encountered during an exercise bout is most likely due to a variety of physiological changes within the exercising muscle. These factors may include lactic acid accumulation, increased tissue acidity, nerve impulse interference, and chemical energy depletion. This type of muscle discomfort is short-lived and quickly dissipates after the exercise bout is completed. Delayed onset muscle soreness (DOMS) is a more lasting form of muscle discomfort. DOMS is usually experienced 24 to 48 hours following an intense or unaccustomed bout of exercise. It is frequently associated with eccentric muscle contractions and is most likely due to microscopic tears in the muscle or connective tissue. For example, when performing the bench press, it isn't pressing the weight up that causes the chest to be sore; it's actually lowering the bar to the chest that makes the exerciser sore.

What causes DOMS? Though the specific cause is unknown, most experts believe that it is caused by microscopic tears in the muscle fibers resulting from the eccentric contraction. Besides pain, DOMS can also involve some swelling, stiffness, and reduction in function.

When athletes begin sprinting programs, the most common area in which they experience DOMS is the hip flexors. These muscles are responsible for lifting up the knees. Most people are not used to picking up their knees when they run. Pain will usually run from approximately midthigh all the way up to the hips. Other areas that might experience DOMS include the hamstrings and the calf muscles.

- What can athletes do to minimize the effects of DOMS?
- Warm up thoroughly: Gradually getting the body ready for exercise will help to minimize DOMS.
- Progress wisely: Remember, athletes have to get in shape and learn the exercises before they can start performing the advanced programs.

If an athlete has DOMS, remind him that it will usually go away on its own within seven to 10 days. If it is severe, you should seriously consider modifying the athlete's workouts until the soreness is gone. Ice and massage will also help.

Quick Tip for Athletes

To minimize delayed onset muscle soreness, warm up thoroughly and ease into the sprinting program.

Shin Splints

Shin splints begin as an annoyance, but can quickly become debilitating. Shin splints involve pain along the tibia. Initially, this pain occurs during sprinting, running, and jumping exercises and usually resolves after the exercise is stopped. As the pain gets worse, it may continue even during rest. Shin splints are thought to be caused by an inability of the tibia to adapt to the exercise and could eventually result in a stress fracture.

What Causes Shin Splints?

Shin splints can be caused by several factors, one of the most common being a sudden increase in training volume. A sudden jump in the amount of sprinting an athlete does will contribute to shin splints. Other potential contributing factors are as follows:

- Running surface: Concrete and turf are terrible surfaces for running sprints and will contribute to shin splints. The best surfaces are grass or a good track.
- Running shoes: Athletes need running shoes that will give them some shock absorption.
- Running mechanics: Running on the toes, or running on the inside or the outside of the foot, will also contribute to shin splints.

- Genetics and the way a person is built: If a person is naturally predisposed to shin splints, the best a coach or athlete can do is control all other factors.

What Can an Athlete Do to Prevent Shin Splints?

The most important thing that a coach or athlete can do to prevent shin splints is to monitor volume increases. Avoid increasing weekly training volume by more than 10 percent per week. For example, if an athlete normally sprints 1000 yards in a week, he should not increase his weekly volume by more than 100 yards. In addition to choosing an appropriate running surface and monitoring training volume, an athlete can do several things to reduce his chances of suffering from shin splints:

- Use proper technique: The athlete must keep his foot cast and land on the balls of his feet when sprinting.
- Strengthen the lower legs: A number of simple exercises can be included at the end of a workout that will be very helpful in preventing shin splints.

Athletes can use these exercises as a cool-down; they take only approximately five minutes. The athlete should pick just one of the following exercises and perform one set as described. He can perform a different exercise at the end of each workout for variety.

- Walking on the toes: For this exercises, the athlete will need 10 to 20 yards of space, preferably on grass. These drills should be done without shoes so that the feet, shins, and ankles have to work to get stronger. The athlete walks on his toes for 10 to 20 yards. Next, he walks on his heels for 10 to 20 yards. Then, he walks on his toes with the toes pointing in (pigeon-toed) for 10 to 20 yards. Then, he walks on his toes with the toes pointing out for 10 to 20 yards. Then, he walks on the inside of his feet for 10 to 20 yards. Finally, he walks on the outside of his feet for 10 to 20 yards.
- Standing on one foot: The athlete may need a partner and a medicine ball for this exercise. Again, this exercise is best done barefoot. The athlete begins by standing on one foot. When he can do this for a minute, he stands on one foot and performs medicine ball chest passes with a partner. When that becomes easy, he stands on one foot and has his partner throw the medicine ball to either side of his shoulders, then his hips, then his knees. Remember, he must stand on one foot. Advanced athletes may perform these same drills standing on an unstable surface, such as a balance disk.
- Simple plyometrics: These exercises are preferably done barefoot. Standing on his toes, the athlete hops forward for 10 to 20 yards. Staying on his toes, he hops backward for 10 to 20 yards. Finally, while still on his toes, he hops in a zigzag pattern for 10 to 20 yards.

- Sand drills: The athlete could perform any of the above exercises, as well as the sprinting technique drills, in the sand while barefoot. The sand will shift under his feet, giving him a great workout.

> **Quick Tip for Athletes**
>
> The following techniques will help prevent shin splints:
>
> - Avoid increasing your training volume by more than 10 percent per week.
> - Sprint on grass or a track.
> - Use proper sprinting technique.
> - Strengthen your lower legs.

What Can an Athlete Do if He Has Shin Splints?

If an athlete has shin splints, the best advice is to have him rest until he is pain free. Complete rest requires avoiding sprinting, jogging, and plyometrics. It is not always possible for an athlete to get this type of rest. Realize, however, that the more he pushes the injury, the more serious it could potentially become.

If the athlete is worried about staying in shape, have him consider sprinting in the pool. This solution is not perfect because the water will interfere with his technique. However, it is better than sitting on the couch. He can perform sprinting-technique drills, bounds, and short sprints in the pool, which will give his tibia a break from the pounding of land-based sprint training. He should be in chest-deep water for this type of exercise.

Pulled Hamstrings

Many people will ignore DOMS and shin splints. Both of these injuries can be worked through, at least in the early stages. But an athlete usually cannot work through a pulled hamstring, which is among the most common injuries in sports.

Pulled hamstrings are characterized by pain in the hamstrings muscles that is often so bad that the athlete will have a limp. A "popping" sensation often accompanies the injury. Swelling and stiffness can also be associated with this type of injury. Athletes who suffer hamstring injuries are more prone to re-injure the area.

Several things could contribute to hamstring injuries. Improper sprinting technique—heel-to-toe running—is a primary cause. Athletes should focus on running on the balls of their feet. Failing to warm up thoroughly will contribute to hamstring injuries as well. Finally, some experts believe that hamstring pulls are more likely if the hamstrings are too weak in comparison to the quadriceps. Strength training should be balanced. Just because an athlete cannot see his hamstrings in the mirror does not mean that they don't require adequate strength training.

A hamstring injury is going to limit itself. Clearly, the injured athlete needs to avoid sprinting if he has a hamstring injury, or symptoms will get worse. After several days of rest, the athlete can ease back into activity. Remind the athlete that it is better to be safe than injure the hamstrings so badly that he needs surgery.

Some common themes behind each of the injuries discussed in this chapter are the importance of warming up properly, utilizing good technique when sprinting, and strengthening the muscles that the athlete will use while sprinting. Following those recommendations and resting when hurt will go a long way toward keeping an athlete healthy. Remember, injured athletes cannot perform at their best.

14

Sample Developmental Programs

Many readers will skip directly to this chapter, which would be a mistake. Doing so means not knowing the "whys" of the training program and instead only getting the "hows." An understanding of the information in the preceding chapters will ensure that your athletes maximize their potential. Those who have read the information in the preceding chapters will know that it is imperative that every athlete starts with the right program. If an athlete hasn't trained in six or more weeks, he will need to start with the varsity program. If he has recently been active and is coming off two or three sport seasons, the All-American program is probably most appropriate. If you are training an athlete who trains year-round, has a collegiate scholarship, and is accustomed to intense physical training, the world class program will likely be most appropriate.

Quick Tip for Athletes

> Choose the right program for you! It is extremely counterproductive to start at a higher-intensity program and then have to back off your training to a lower intensity.

The Varsity Program

Use the following prerequisites to determine if the varsity program is right for a specific athlete:

- He hasn't trained in six or more weeks.
- He is just beginning to train for the first time in his career.
- He only has two days per week to work on the 40.

- He is coming off an injury, but is healthy and cleared to participate.
- He often overestimates his physical condition.
- He fully anticipates getting sore and tired during the first week or two of practice.
- He has only two to four weeks to train and needs some fundamental training.

The varsity program involves training two days per week, either Monday and Thursday or Tuesday and Friday. An athlete could also train on Wednesday and Saturday or Sunday. The idea is to complete two training days per week with two or three days of rest between workouts. Training specifically for the 40 twice per week should net some significant results.

On both training days, the starting stance technique and the drive phase are emphasized. Again, these elements are essential to running the best time. The acceleration phase is added on the second day and distances of 40 yards are reached. Nothing beyond 40 yards is worth training in the varsity program for two reasons: training top speed beyond 40 yards is not required and athletes will get the greatest results from focusing on the start, drive, and acceleration phases.

Remind athletes to pay particular attention to the rest intervals, which means that you and the rest of your coaching staff—or the athletes themselves—will need to bring watches. After sprinting short distances, it is important that each athlete gets his nervous system fully restored before the next repetition. Figure 14-1 presents all components of the varsity program, while Figure 14-2 presents a four-day-a-week program that combines strength training and agility training with the varsity program.

Quick Tip for Athletes

If you shorten the rest intervals, you will run more slowly because you will be in a fatigued state. Ultimately, running slowly only trains your body to run slowly.

Quick Tip for Athletes

Most athletes both lift weights and run during the off-season. If you want to maximize your 40-yard time, *run first, then lift*.

All-American Program

Use the following prerequisites to determine if the All-American program is right for a specific athlete:

- He is a two- or three-sport athlete.
- He has been through several off-seasons.

	Monday or Tuesday	Thursday or Friday
Training Objectives	Starting stance technique Drive phase	Starting stance technique Drive phase Acceleration phase
General Warm-Up	5–10 minutes	5–10 minutes
Dynamic Warm-Up	5–10 minutes	5–10 minutes
Form-Running Drills	Arm swings Ankling Heel kicks High knee A drill	Arm swings Ankling Heel kicks High knee A drill
Distance/Repetitions	5 yards/8 reps 15 yards/6 reps	5 yards/5 reps 20 yards/5 reps 40 yards/3 reps
Rest Interval	3 minutes between all reps 5 minutes when transitioning between distances	3 minutes between all reps 5 minutes when transitioning between distances

Figure 14-1. The varsity program

Monday	Tuesday	Thursday	Friday
40-yard training as described Figure 14-1	Upper-body strength training: bench press, pull-ups, abdominal workout	40-yard training as described in Figure 14-1	Upper-body strength training: dumbbell bench press, dumbbell rows, abdominals workout
Lower-body strength training: cleans, squats, Romanian dead lifts	Agility training	Lower-body strength training: snatches, front squats, Romanian dead lifts	Agility training

Figure 14-2. Four-day-a-week program combining agility and strength training with the varsity program

- He is ready to try incorporating plyometric training.
- He has three days per week to work on the 40.
- He is a scholarship athlete or hopeful and in good condition.
- He clearly understands and has trained the fundamentals of the start, drive phase, and top speed.

- He fully anticipates not getting sore and tired during the first week or two of practice.
- He has been very active for several weeks, including lifting weights and performing structured running and conditioning.
- He has four to six weeks to train and needs to ramp up his training.

The three-day-per-week program presented as Monday/Wednesday/Friday in Figures 14-3 through 14-5 can be "shifted" one day earlier or later in the week, effectively making the training days Sunday/Tuesday/Thursday or Tuesday/Thursday/Saturday. The training is set up in three two-week blocks. The repetitions, distances, and plyometrics all progress over the six weeks. If an athlete takes his time and gives this program his best effort, the results should be phenomenal.

	Monday	Wednesday	Friday
Training Objectives	Starting stance technique Drive phase	Acceleration phase Top speed phase	Starting stance technique Drive phase
General Warm-Up	5–10 minutes	5–10 minutes	5–10 minutes
Dynamic Warm-Up	5–10 minutes	5–10 minutes	5–10 minutes
Form-Running Drills	Arm swings Ankling Heel kicks High knee A drill	Arm swings Ankling Heel kicks High knee A drill	Arm swings Ankling Heel kicks High knee A drill
Distance/Repetitions	5 yards/8 reps 15 yards/6 reps	5 yards/5 reps 20 yards/5 reps 40 yards/3 reps	5 yards/8 reps 15 yards/6 reps
Rest Interval	3 minutes between all reps 5 minutes when transitioning between distances	3 minutes between all reps 5 minutes when transitioning between distances	3 minutes between all reps 5 minutes when transitioning between distances
Plyometrics (sets x reps)	Double-leg hops, single response 3x6 Power skips 2x30 yards	Box jumps 3x6 90/90 touches 3x5	Double-leg hops, single response 3x6 Power skips 2x30 yards

Figure 14-3. All-American program, weeks 1 and 2

	Monday	Wednesday	Friday
Training Objectives	Starting stance technique Drive phase	Acceleration phase Top speed phase	Starting stance technique Drive phase
General Warm-Up	5–10 minutes	5–10 minutes	5–10 minutes
Dynamic Warm-Up	5–10 minutes	5–10 minutes	5–10 minutes
Form-Running Drills	Arm swings Ankling Heel kicks High knee A drill	Arm swings Ankling Heel kicks High knee A drill	Arm swings Ankling Heel kicks High knee A drill
Distance/Repetitions	10 yards/8 reps 25 yards/6 reps	20 yards/4 reps 40 yards/4 reps 60 yards/4 reps	10 yards/8 reps 25 yards/6 reps
Rest Interval	3 minutes between all reps 5 minutes when transitioning between distances	3 minutes between all reps 5 minutes when transitioning between distances	3 minutes between all reps 5 minutes when transitioning between distances
Plyometrics (sets x reps)	Double-leg hops over cones 3x6 Power skips 2x30 yards	Box jumps 3x6 90/90 touches 3x5 Step-up jumps 3x6	Double-leg hops over cones 3x6 Power skips 2x30 yards

Figure 14-4. All-American program, weeks 3 and 4

If an athlete is serious enough to take six weeks to prepare to run the 40, he will most likely be lifting and using agility/conditioning as part of his program as well. Figure 14-6 provides a five-day-per-week training schedule that combines lifting, plyometrics, and agility/conditioning.

World Class Program

Use the following prerequisites to determine if the world class program is right for a specific athlete:

- He is a collegiate or professional athlete.
- He has been through several off-seasons.
- He has used plyometric training for several years.
- He has four days per week to work on the 40.

	Monday	Wednesday	Friday
Training Objectives	Starting stance technique Drive phase	Acceleration phase Top speed phase	Starting stance technique Drive phase
General Warm-Up	5–10 minutes	5–10 minutes	5–10 minutes
Dynamic Warm-Up	5–10 minutes	5–10 minutes	5–10 minutes
Form-Running Drills	Arm swings Ankling Heel kicks High knee A drill	Arm swings Ankling Heel kicks High knee A drill	Arm swings Ankling Heel kicks High knee A drill
Distance/Repetitions	15 yards/8 reps 30 yards/6 reps	20 yards/4 reps 40 yards/8 reps	10 yards/8 reps 25 yards/6 reps
Rest Interval	3 minutes between all reps 5 minutes when transitioning between distances	3 minutes between all reps 5 minutes when transitioning between distances	3 minutes between all reps 5 minutes when transitioning between distances
Plyometrics (sets x reps)	Double-leg hops over cones 3x6 Power skips 2x30 yards	Box jumps 3x6 90/90 touches 3x5 Step-up jumps 3x6	Double-leg hops over cones 3x6 Power skips 2x30 yards

Figure 14-5. All-American program, weeks 5 and 6

Monday	Tuesday	Wednesday	Thursday	Friday
40-yard training as described in Figures 14-3 through 14-5	Agility training	40-yard training as described in Figures 14-3 through 14-5	Agility training	40-yard training as described in Figures 14-3 through 14-5
Lower-body strength training: cleans squats, and Romanian dead lifts	Upper-body strength training: bench press, pull-ups, abdominal training		Lower-body strength training: cleans squats, and Romanian dead lifts	Upper-body strength training: bench press, pull-ups, abdomina training

Figure 14-6. Five-day-a-week program combining agility and strength training with the All-American program

- He is a collegiate or postcollegiate athlete and in good condition.
- He clearly understands and has trained the fundamentals of the starting phase, drive phase, and top speed.
- He fully anticipates *not* getting sore and tired during the first week or two of practice.
- He has been very active for several weeks, including lifting weights and performing structured running and conditioning.
- He has six to eight weeks to train and needs to ramp up his training.

Quick Tip for Athletes

Adhere to the progression presented for the program you choose. Skipping weeks is a recipe for failure.

The world class program is built around four days a week of speed training. Monday and Thursday focus on taking the first few steps as explosively as possible. Tuesday and Friday focus on maximal speed. The warm-ups are longer than in the varsity or All-American programs, because the workouts are more intense, which means that athletes will need more time to prepare for the workouts. Notice also that the warm-ups are longest during the maximal speed days.

During the maximal speed days, faster and more explosive form-running drills are included. These drills should be done as part of the dynamic warm-up, because by this point the techniques should be ingrained. As a result, the warm-up drills can be done at a faster pace and at speeds that more closely resemble real-life conditions.

As in the varsity and All-American programs, each workout starts with five-yard sprints, which should be done from the appropriate stance. These five-yard sprints are done as a transition between warming up and working out and to help the athlete focus on taking the first step explosively.

Remember, due to the greater complexity and intensity of the workouts, the rest periods are longer than in the other two programs. Therefore, the workouts will take longer. Remember, quality is more important than doing the workouts exactly as they are written. Plyometrics are still being performed to emphasize getting off the ground explosively, exerting force against the ground, and achieving vertical distance.

Quick Tip for Athletes

If you slow down or if your technique breaks down, then you should stop the workout.

Weeks 1 and 2

Monday's workouts during weeks 1 and 2 are pretty similar to those in the other programs. The athlete transitions into the program with five-yard sprints, emphasizing taking that first step as explosively as possible and accelerating for those five yards. The 20-yard sprints should reinforce good starting technique and teach the athlete how to cover those 20 yards as quickly as possible.

Tuesday's workouts focus on maximal speed. Five-yard sprints are still performed to transition into the workout. However, Tuesday's workout focuses on "ins and outs" done over 60 yards, as shown in Figure 14-7.

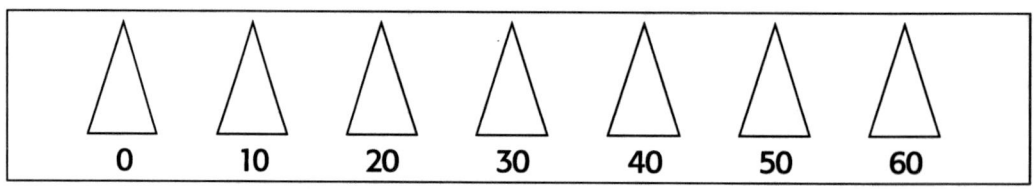

Figure 14-7. 60-yard ins and outs

Thursday's workout again focuses on the first few steps. However, after the five-yard sprints, the athlete should perform 20-yard sprints against resistance while focusing on technique and moving as quickly as possible. Make sure the athlete then completes the 20-yard sprints without resistance.

Friday's workouts continue to focus on maximal speed. Sprints are done for 60 yards, during which the athlete should focus on technique, speed, and running through the last cone. Figure 14-8 presents the workout schedule for weeks 1 and 2.

Weeks 3 and 4

Weeks 3 and 4 are a continuation of, and expansion on, the first two weeks (Figure 14-9). The workouts are organized in the same manner. However, the volume increases as the athlete adjusts to the workouts, to make them more difficult. Notice that the distances run on Friday also increase.

Weeks 5 and 6

Weeks 5 and 6 introduce some small changes to the workouts (Figure 14-10). Monday and Thursday remain the same as they were during the previous four weeks. The changes come on the maximum speed days—Tuesday and Friday. Tuesday involves performing "flying" 40-yard sprints, which involve taking 10 yards to accelerate, then running as fast as possible for the remaining 40 (i.e., a 10-yard acceleration zone, then a 40-yard maximum-speed zone). The athlete should focus on technique and speed during these sprints. Friday's workouts also involve 100-yard sprints. Again, the athlete should focus on technique, because he can quickly get tired and sloppy during these drills.

	Monday	Tuesday	Thursday	Friday
Training Objectives	Starting stance technique Drive phase	Acceleration phase Top speed phase	Starting stance technique Drive phase	Acceleration phase Top speed phase
General Warm-Up	5–10 minutes	5–10 minutes	5–10 minutes	5–10 minutes
Dynamic Warm-Up	10–15 minutes	15–20 minutes	10–15 minutes	10–20 minutes
Form-Running Drills	Ankling Heel kicks High knee A drill	Straight-leg bounds Heel kicks run High-knee skips A skips	Ankling Heel kicks High knee A drill	Straight-leg bounds Heel kicks run High-knee skips A skips
Distance/ Repetitions	5 yards/8 reps 20 yards/6 reps	5 yards/4 reps Ins and outs, 60 yards/5 reps	5 yards/8 reps 20 yards resisted/6 reps 20 yards/6 reps	5 yards/4 reps 60 yards/5 reps
Rest Interval	3 minutes between all reps 5 minutes when transitioning between distances	3 minutes between all reps 5 minutes between the 5-yard sprints and the ins and outs distances	3 minutes between all reps 5 minutes when transitioning between distances	3 minutes between the 5-yard reps 5 minutes between the 60-yard reps 5 minutes when transitioning between distances
Plyometrics (sets x reps)	Double-leg hops over cones 3x6 Power skips 2x30 yards	Box jumps 3x6 90/90 touches 3x5 Step-up jumps 3x6	Double-leg hops over cones 3x6 Power skips 2x30 yards	Box jumps 3x6 90/90 touches 3x5 Step-up jumps 3x6

Figure 14-8. World class program, weeks 1 and 2

Weeks 7 and 8

During the last two weeks of this program, the structure remains the same, though some small changes take place. First, volume is still increasing as the athlete gets adjusted to the program. Second, Friday's workout is a little different than in the previous six weeks. Friday's workouts involve running resisted 40-yard sprints (for example, with a parachute). It is very important that the athlete focuses on perfect technique and running quickly during the resisted sprints, otherwise these runs will be detrimental. After performing the resisted sprints, the athlete must perform them without resistance. He should notice a difference and feel lighter (i.e., faster) when doing the sprints without resistance. A five-day–per-week training schedule that combines lifting, plyometrics, and agility is presented in Figure 14-12.

	Monday	Tuesday	Thursday	Friday
Training Objectives	Starting stance technique Drive phase	Acceleration phase Top speed phase	Starting stance technique Drive phase	Acceleration phase Top speed phase
General Warm-Up	5–10 minutes	5–10 minutes	5–10 minutes	5–10 minutes
Dynamic Warm-Up	10–15 minutes	15–20 minutes	10–15 minutes	10–20 minutes
Form-Running Drills	Ankling Heel kicks High knee A drill	Straight-leg bounds Heel kicks run High-knee skips A skips	Ankling Heel kicks High knee A drill	Straight-leg bounds Heel kicks run High-knee skips A skips
Distance/ Repetitions	5 yards/8 reps 20 yards/7 reps	5 yards/4 reps Ins and outs, 60 yards/6 reps	5 yards/8 reps 20 yards resisted/6 reps 20 yards/7 reps	5 yards/4 reps 75 yards/5 reps
Rest Interval	3 minutes between all reps 5 minutes when transitioning between distances	3 minutes between all reps 5 minutes between the 5-yard sprints and the ins and outs distances	3 minutes between all reps 5 minutes when transitioning between distances	3 minutes between the 5-yard reps 5 minutes between the 75-yard reps 5 minutes when transitioning between distances
Plyometrics (sets x reps)	Double-leg hops over cones 3x6 Power skips 2x30 yards	Box jumps 3x6 90/90 touches 3x5 Step-up jumps 3x6	Double-leg hops over cones 3x6 Power skips 2x30 yards	Box jumps 3x6 90/90 touches 3x5 Step-up jumps 3x6

Figure 14-9. World class program, weeks 3 and 4

	Monday	Tuesday	Thursday	Friday
Training Objectives	Starting stance technique Drive phase	Acceleration phase Top speed phase	Starting stance technique Drive phase	Acceleration phase Top speed phase
General Warm-Up	5–10 minutes	5–10 minutes	5–10 minutes	5–10 minutes
Dynamic Warm-Up	10–15 minutes	15–20 minutes	10–15 minutes	10–20 minutes
Form-Running Drills	Ankling Heel kicks High knee A drill	Straight-leg bounds Heel kicks run High-knee skips A skips	Ankling Heel kicks High knee A drill	Straight-leg bounds Heel kicks run High-knee skips A skips
Distance/ Repetitions	5 yards/8 reps 20 yards/6 reps	5 yards/4 reps Flying 40s/8 reps	5 yards/8 reps 20 yards resisted/6 reps 20 yards/6 reps	5 yards/4 reps 60 yards/5 reps
Rest Interval	3 minutes between all reps 5 minutes when transitioning between distances	3 minutes between all reps 5 minutes between flying 40s 5 minutes when transitioning between distances	3 minutes between all reps 5 minutes when transitioning between distances	3 minutes between the 5-yard reps 5 minutes between the 60-yard reps 5 minutes when transitioning between distances
Plyometrics (sets x reps)	Double-leg hops over cones 3x6 Power skips 2x30 yards	Box jumps 3x6 90/90 touches 3x5 Step-up jumps 3x6	Double-leg hops over cones 3x6 Power skips 2x30 yards	Box jumps 3x6 90/90 touches 3x5 Step-up jumps 3x6

Figure 14-10. World class program, weeks 5 and 6

	Monday	Tuesday	Thursday	Friday
Training Objectives	Starting stance technique Drive phase	Acceleration phase Top speed phase	Starting stance technique Drive phase	Acceleration phase Top speed phase
General Warm-Up	5–10 minutes	5–10 minutes	5–10 minutes	5–10 minutes
Dynamic Warm-Up	10–15 minutes	15–20 minutes	10–15 minutes	10–20 minutes
Form-Running Drills	Ankling Heel kicks High knee A drill	Straight-leg bounds Heel kicks run High-knee skips A skips	Ankling Heel kicks High knee A drill	Straight-leg bounds Heel kicks run High-knee skips A skips
Distance/ Repetitions	5 yards/8 reps 20 yards/6 reps	5 yards/4 reps Flying 40s/8 reps	5 yards/8 reps 20 yards resisted/6 reps 20 yards/6 reps	5 yards/4 reps 40 yards resisted/5 reps 40 yards/5 reps
Rest Interval	3 minutes between all reps 5 minutes when transitioning between distances	3 minutes between 5-yard reps 5 minutes between flying 40s 5 minutes when transitioning between distances	3 minutes between all reps 5 minutes when transitioning between distances	3 minutes between the 5-yard reps 5 minutes between the 40-yard reps 5 minutes between 40-yard resisted reps 5 minutes when transitioning between distances
Plyometrics (sets x reps)	Double-leg hops over cones 3x6 Power skips 2x30 yards	Box jumps 3x6 90/90 touches 3x5 Step-up jumps 3x6	Double-leg hops over cones 3x6 Power skips 2x30 yards	Box jumps 3x6 90/90 touches 3x5 Step-up jumps 3x6

Figure 14-11. World class program, weeks 7 and 8

Monday	Tuesday	Wednesday	Thursday	Friday
40-yard training as described in Figures 14-9 through 14-11	40-yard training as described in Figures 14-9 through 14-11		40-yard training as described in Figures 14-9 through 14-11	40-yard training as described in Figures 14-9 through 14-11
Lower-body strength training: cleans squats, and Romanian dead lifts	Agility Training	Upper-body strength training: bench press, pull-ups, abdominal training	Agility Training	Total-body strength training: snatches, front squats, bench press, pull-ups, abdominal training

Figure 14-12. Five-day-a-week program combining lifting, plyometrics, and agility with the world class program

Summary

The programs presented in this chapter combine every aspect of speed training that has been covered in this book. Remember that when an athlete is training for speed, it must be his top priority. Lifting weights, agility training, and plyometrics are all great forms of exercise, but they are not substitutes for speed training. Mastering running technique helps to make an athlete faster and prevents injuries. Also, remember to have each athlete follow the appropriate workout program and progress slowly.

About the Authors

Michael Barnes is the owner of Infinity Personal Training and Fitness. He has been a strength and conditioning practitioner and educator in the field for more than 15 years. He holds a master's degree in health and human performance from Auburn University and certifications from the National Strength and Conditioning Association (Certified Strength and Conditioning Specialist with Distinction and Certified Personal Trainer with Distinction) and the International Society on Sports Nutrition (Certified Sports Nutritionist).

Michael has coordinated books and videos and has presented at many conferences on strength and conditioning. Projects in which he has participated include work done with USA Cycling, USA Judo, USA Rugby, the National Athletic Trainers Association, the National Strength and Conditioning Association, the American College of Sports Medicine, and the United States Marine Corps.

Michael's past experience includes six years with the San Francisco 49ers as their strength development coordinator. He has traveled the world, visiting such places as Japan, Australia, Puerto Rico, Bermuda, Greece, and Denmark, educating and training athletes and interacting with leaders in the fitness industry.

John Cissik is the director of fitness and recreation at Texas Woman's University and is the owner of Fitness and Conditioning Enterprises, which specializes in providing speed and agility instruction to young athletes. John also serves as strength and conditioning consultant with several track and field teams.

John holds a master's degree in kinesiology from Texas A&M University and several certifications from the National Strength and Conditioning Association (Certified Strength and Conditioning Specialist with Distinction, NSCA-Certified Personal Trainer with Distinction), USA Track and Field (Level II Coach – Sprints, Level I Coach), and USA Weightlifting (Club Coach).

John has been very active in the strength and conditioning field for a number of years. He has held a variety of positions, from coaching to teaching to personal training. He has written several books on strength and speed training, as well as many coaching and lay articles, has done several videos, and has given many presentations. He has served as a reviewer for the NSCA's *Strength and Conditioning Journal*, as well as several of its educational products. He also served as the NSCA's State Director for Texas from 2001–2004.